The Hidden Meaning of Mass Communications

The Hidden Meaning of Mass Communications

Cinema, Books, and Television in the Age of Computers

FEREYDOUN HOVEYDA

Westport, Connecticut
London

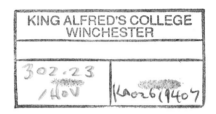
Library of Congress Cataloging-in-Publication Data

Hoveyda, Fereydoun.
    The hidden meaning of mass communications : cinema, books, and
television in the age of computers / Fereydoun Hoveyda.
        p.   cm.
    Includes bibliographical references and index.
    ISBN 0–275–96996–7 (alk. paper)
        1. Mass media.   2. Mass media—Technological innovations.   I. Title.
    P91.H677   2000
    302.23—dc21   00–022832

British Library Cataloguing in Publication Data is available.

Library of Congress Catalog Card Number: 00–022832
ISBN: 0–275–96996–7

First published in 2000

Praeger Publishers, 88 Post Road West, Westport, CT 06881
An imprint of Greenwood Publishing Group, Inc.
www.praeger.com

Printed in the United States of America

The paper used in this book complies with the
Permanent Paper Standard issued by the National
Information Standards Organization (Z39.48–1984).

10 9 8 7 6 5 4 3 2

All illustrations are from the author's private collection.

Contents

Photo essay follows page 79.

Acknowledgments

I want to thank Dudley Andrew, the distinguished director of the cinema department at the University of Iowa at Iowa City and the author of the remarkable biography of my late friend André Bazin, co-founder of *Cahiers du Cinéma*. Indeed, our discussions and his kind invitation to me to address his students in November 1998 rekindled memories of my participation in the battles for an "auteur" cinema in Paris in the late 1950s. Upon my return from Iowa, I toyed for some time with the idea of writing about that period of my life and about what I think of film, books and mass communications today. Finally, in March 1999, I sat in front of the word processor screen.

I must also thank Dr. Sabin and his colleagues at Praeger Publishers for accepting my manuscript. I also want to express my gratitude to Ms. Christine Farrugia and all the editors of Greenwood for their untiring efforts in improving both the text and the presentation of this book, my second fully written in English.

Introduction: Cinema and Books

One 1930 Saturday afternoon, I accompanied my mother and brother to a theater showing *Ben Hur*. Although talkies had already come to Beirut, silent hits continued to be shown in the multicultural Lebanese capital, especially when they contained footage about Jesus. Overwhelmed by the action-packed feature, I remained glued to the silver screen until the very end and heartily participated in the applause that erupted as the curtain fell. (Indeed, Fred Niblo's production was excellent and some of its episodes, such as the naval battle and the chariot race, still hold their own compared to contemporary digitally supported and overbudgeted "historical" extravaganzas.) On our way home, my brother, who was my elder by five years, explained: "This is exactly the book!" I couldn't believe my ears until, the next day, when he brought back from his class library the Lew Wallace novel.

This incident captured my imagination. Films equated with books! An extraordinary idea dawned in my mind: Films could replace books! "What the heck do I care?" I thought to myself. "No more tedious classrooms! Schools will soon look like cinemas where, instead of reading books, kids will learn directly from the screen!" I was in second grade, painfully struggling with grammar, spelling, and vocabulary, while images on the screen spoke instantly to me, without any previous preparation! I had already learned a lot about geography, history, psychology, words, and expressions from films. I knew Hugo's *Les Misérables*, Shakespeare's *Romeo and Juliet*, Dumas's *Three Musketeers*, Dickens's *Oliver Twist*, and some other literary masterpieces. Cinema was also an uncomparable window on the world. At age six I became familiar with exotic locales in the Pacific as well as fabulous countries of the East and West: China, Japan, America, France, England, Germany, Russia, and so on. ... Beyond geography, politics also penetrated my world through newsreels. I could recognize England's king, George V, Italy's Mussolini, Russia's Stalin, Japan's Hirohito, and the like. I watched with amazement as riots, strikes, local wars, and other forms of mayhem filled the screen. I even learned a lot about America's conquest of the West through Tom Mix's westerns! I did not understand my brother's appetite for books, a form of transfer of knowledge I already considered obsolete! I envisioned a world in which "moving images" would replace written and printed words. Writers would use a movie camera instead of a pen[1] and education would spread instantly all over the planet! But as the years passed, nothing of the sort happened and my former enthusiastic hopes gradually evaporated. Although I never surrendered to our teachers' contention about the so-called superiority of books over films, I came to look at cinema as sheer *entertainment*.

Later on, I completely forgot my childhood musings about a "filmic" revolution in education. After completing my studies, I settled in Paris and became an assiduous patron of the recently founded "Cinématheque" (Film Library) where Henri Langlois[2] showed his collections of pre-war European and American movies. I also read a lot and occasionally witnessed discussions between writers and filmmakers about the unique advantages of their respective crafts. One day I found in a 1917 Guillaume Apollinaire interview the following assertion: "[Books] will die in one or two centuries. They will be succeeded by phonographic disks and cinematographic films. People will not need to read or write anymore."[3] This remark awakened in my mind the forgotten memory of my childhood's wool gatherings. I was baffled: Early in the century, when cinema and recordings were still in their infancy, the great French poet had sounded the death knell of books *only a few years before me*! I felt somehow proud of this coincidence!

Yet, after almost a century, Apollinaire's prophecy (mine, too!) has not yet come true. I wonder what his reactions would have been to the current technological revolution that is sweeping the fields of information and communications. He would probably have felt vindicated to some extent, if not completely. Indeed, television and other audiovisual innovations have steadily eaten into the time people devote to reading. Even newspapers and magazines have lost many readers.

The least one can say is that the satellite, computer, and Internet age, which is just dawning on humanity, has already produced a notable change in our habits and cultural environment. They have not only accentuated the shift from book to screen, but caused a visible switch from print to what might be called a "digital culture." Nevertheless, old debates about books and films die hard and continue to pit the literary establishment against the rising audiovisual crowd. On top of that, the unceasing flow of technological inventions in the field of communications worries governments and educators. In open, democratic societies, politicians and private organizations decry the access of children to "unfit" material. In less-developed countries, the free flow of information threatens authoritarian leaders and frightens traditionalists and conservatives. The latter denounce "Western cultural invasion," while the former see a direct threat to their grip on power.

All these bickerings blur and obfuscate the discussions concerning the future of books and films in the new electronic Information Age. Are we really witnessing the end of the "Gutenberg Galaxy" (Marshall McLuhan)? Will books "die" (Apollinaire)? Are we entering a new age in the fields of communications and entertainment? To find answers to such questions, it seems useful to try to evaluate the reciprocal influences of films and literature on each other, as well as the impact of new technologies on both of them. We should also debunk a number of false contentions and assertions from the past and present.

1

Superiority of Literature?

For most of the twentieth century, many writers treated films with contempt and viewed cinema with disdain. Perhaps, George Bernard Shaw's humorous views, expressed in a 1937 letter, epitomize them all:

> I sat out a film [*The General Died at Dawn*] in which Gary Cooper and Madeline [*sic*] Carroll kept having their photographs taken for an hour or so ... The photographs were very good, and the lighting and scenery first rate ... It was really beautifully done; and it held the audience as a picture book holds a child.... I left the theater without the faintest notion of what it was all about. I could not make out why Gary Cooper socked those innocent and picturesque people on the jaw. As to Madeline, her transitions from being a virtuous heroine to being a crook's decoy were so bewildering that Cooper at last socked her on the jaw without affecting in the least her infatuation for him. From time to time they made inarticulate noises with American accents, with all the consonants left out. Not one word could I understand, nor could Charlotte.... Now set your analytical faculty, if you have any, to tabulate all the techniques involved in these extraordinary exhibitions....

Up to a certain point it pays. Most of the studios seem to
live by it. But in such studios the dramatist can find no
place. They know that they can do without him. Nevertheless, they sent a boy to Whitehall Court for the "rights" of
The Devil's Disciple. If they got them they would make a
picture book of the play. The picture book might be a very
gorgeous one. Dick would be very handsome; and the
close-up of Uncle Titus and Uncle William would suggest
all the characters in America's darkest fiction Judith's eyebrows would be shaved off and replaced by a proper Hollywood pair. Burgoyne surrendering to Gates on the field
of Saratoga and marching out proudly with the honors of
war would provide a glorious spectacular finish. All the
scenery of New England would be used up in the transformation of my five little scenes into five hundred. An-
derson will die at Saratoga and stain an anachronistic Old
Glory with his blood, leaving Judith to fall into Dick's arms
and make him unhappy for ever after. And nobody at the
end would have the faintest notion of what it was all about.
They don't even know, poor devils, that there is such a
thing as a dramatic technique. Get drama and picture making separate in your mind, or you may make ruinous mis-
takes.[4]

So much for the sound cinema. Let's turn to Hermann Hesse
for the silents. While in Baden for a cure in the mid-1920s, he
stepped into a film theater. He consigned his anger to his *Autobiographical Writings* (New York, 1973) as follows:

For hours I watched a film about an ancient empress unroll,
complete with theater, circus, church, gladiators, lions,
saints and eunuchs. I sat there and watched while the highest values and symbols (the throne and scepter, vestments
and halos, cross and imperial globe) together with all possible and impossible qualities and conditions of the soul, and
men and animals by the hundreds were summoned up for
laughable reasons and put on show; this potentially splen-
did display was degraded by interminable, completely idi-
otic subtitles, and poisoned by false dramatization, and

disgraced and cheapened by a heartless and headless public (I too am part of it). . . . I watched the trash to its end.

Now for the present, some fifty years after Shaw, John Updike
had this to say:

> [Filmmakers] bring their vision to market through a welter
> of props and egos, actors and bankers that a mere word-
> monger would be overwhelmed by. Considering the vast
> number of fingers in the pot, and the amount of financial
> concern that haunts the sound stage, it's a wonder any mo-
> tion picture comes out halfway coherent. Lack of coher-
> ence—the inner coherence works of art should have, the
> simplicity of one voice speaking—is surely a failing espe-
> cially of today's films, in the absence of studio control and
> of the adult bourgeois audience that filled the movie pal-
> aces in the Palmy Depression days. Now, only adolescents
> have strong and recurrent reason to go out of the house . . .
> Even a very lame movie tends to crush a book . . . Who can
> now read *For Whom the Bell Tolls* and not visualize the trav-
> elling hero as an avatar of Sergeant York or its Spanish
> virgin as a Swedish beauty?[5]

Evidently, not all writers shared Shaw's, Hesse's, or Updike's
contempt. The French surrealists and a number of young novelists all over the world looked enthusiastically at movies.

> V. S. Naipaul in an article titled "The Writer and India"
> declares: "Nearly all my imaginative life (as a child) was
> in the cinema. Everything there was far away, but at the
> same time everything in that curious operatic world was
> accessible. It was truly a universal art I don't think I over-
> state when I say that without the Hollywood of the 1930s
> and 1940s I would have been spiritually quite destitute.
> That cannot be shut out of this account of reading and writ-
> ing. And I have to wonder now whether the talent that
> once went into imaginative literature didn't in this century

go into the first fifty years of the glorious cinema." (*The New York Review of Books*, March 4, 1999)

But, in general, most of them seemed to misunderstand films. For example, Jean-Paul Sartre had seen *Citizen Kane* in 1945 in New York. Upon his return to Paris, he condemned its "pretentiousness" in *L'Ecran Français* (August 1945) and suggested that it was flawed aesthetically! Jorge Luis Borges, who practiced film criticism in Buenos Aires in the 1930s, showed a similar obtuseness in his reviews! Moreover, many established authors did not hide their disdain. Thus, I remember reading in the Arts section of a 1971 Sunday edition of the *New York Times*, a long article from which I copied the following few sentences into my personal notebook (alas without mention of the precise publication date):

> Film demonstrates that words do the job of storytelling far better. *The Exorcist* is a wretched enough book, God or the devil knows, but it is still superior to the film. The book persuades one to take demonic possession seriously, while the film makes a joke of it. . . . But let us consider works of literature, which the film world thinks its duty to continue to try to drag screaming into the light, despite long evidence of inconvertibility. . . . I first saw *The Great Gatsby* . . . The book has style while the film is merely stylish . . . One of the mysterious laws underlying film adaptation seems to be this: director may be inferior to author, director may be superior to author, but director may not be equal to author. Find a film director with the esthetic and moral authority of Henry James, and you may get a good Henry James film. But such a man would prefer not to interpret another artist, but to create his own art. The great filmmakers do not bring literature to screen. The worlds of Buñuel, Fellini and Godard are totally unbookish . . . It all comes back to words. This is why literature is superior to the other arts and, indeed, why there can be a hierarchy of arts. . . . Film, seeming to have all resources, and more of literature, still cannot produce anything as a great work

of literature. . . . The light and shade and downright darkness of my language cannot, however brilliant the director,
find a cinematic analogue . . . Film is more limited than
prose fiction.

These lines were written by Anthony Burgess who, at the time,
had won international fame because of Stanley Kubrick's movie
based on Burgess's book, *A Clockwork Orange*. I have quoted
them here because they express, in my opinion, some of the
prejudices of the literary establishment against cinema.

As a rule, most writers regard films as a school for intellectual
laziness. To them, the first place belongs to literature, an "aristo-
cratic" art that is chronologically first and boasts a long tradition.
It is precisely here that they are wrong! Literature is not chronologically first. Cinema existed long before articulate speech appeared. Image, still or animated, goes back to the very
beginnings of mankind. It preceded every other means of communication, including the first stumbling efforts at articulate
speech. In saying this, I am not indulging in some game of paradox. Indeed, in order to justify my proposition, it is enough to
reflect for a moment on prehistoric cave drawings and especially
on what we know of the phenomena of nocturnal dreams and
waking fantasies. Inasmuch as the experts agree that dreaming
is directly connected with sleep, it does not seem rash to suppose
that humans have always had dreams. The oldest written
traditions inform us of the keen interest people took in this nocturnal activity of their brains. Since the most remote antiquity,
these fugitive images have seemed so strongly to conceal hidden
meanings that the princes and potentates of those times always
maintained "patented" interpreters in their retinues while the
masses resorted to the *Keys to Dreams* compiled by the sages or
to cheap bazaar soothsayers.

2

Cinema and Dreams

We had to wait until the last years of the nineteenth century for access at last to a systematic study of the phenomenon of dreams. Freud explained that dreams possess a structure of their own and a particular significant concatenation of images (*The Interpretation of Dreams*, English translation, New York, 1950). They are the end product of an evolutionary process that transforms their "latent" content into "manifest" content. He called this transformation process "dream work" and catalogued and described the mechanisms by which it occurs. These mechanisms are: distortion and displacement; symbolization (figuration); condensation; and secondary elaboration. Now, these operations, which take place simultaneously in the dreamer's unconscious, are curiously reminiscent of the techniques of literary and cinematic narratives. Thus, symbolization (figuration) performs the selection and transformation that makes it possible to represent the dream's "thoughts" in primary visual images. It is a process of the same kind as the work done by filmmakers on the scenario in order to make a "shooting script" out of it. Similarly, the secondary elaboration, which in the dream consists of relieving it of apparent absurdity, filling its gaps, and subjecting it to both selection and addition, is astonishingly close to the techniques of editing and cutting in. As for the other mechanisms, they are part of all forms of literary or cinematic narrative, so I shall not belabor the point. Moreover, many of the "modern" innovations in film style already existed in dreams discontinuity, jumps in plot and scene location, jump-cuts, etc! In a way dreamers can be compared to creative artists.

The most remarkable thing about dreams is that dreamers perform all the functions and roles of an entire film crew. They are simultaneously scenarist, director, actor, art director, dress stylist, editor, and, last but not least, audience! (All of that without having attended a film or acting school!) In other words, dreamers are the complete "authors" of their dreams. In contrast to filmmakers, they do not enjoy the cooperation of a host of technicians and specialists. The end product of their nocturnal activity is entirely and in all its aspects the result of their own personal efforts. To be sure, they borrow material from their environment and their daily experiences. But they choose, transform, and combine them according to their mood and fantasy. Their dreams, therefore, represent their typical mode of expression, their characteristic tone, their personal way of narration, in a word, their *style*. Their "personality" (character) and preoccupations emerge in their "style," in the manner in which they "narrate" a dream, not in its subject matter.[6] Curiously enough, when analyzing dreams, interpreters, including most psychoanalysts and psychologists, overlook the "style" in favor of the "scenario," the "narration manner" in favor of the "subject." They ignore the genuine "directorial" technique that frames the dream and reveals its true meaning. This aspect of the dream eluded Freud completely. Consider his emphasis on the "noncreative" character of the "dream work" on the grounds that dreams merely transform pre-existing raw materials—as if matters were any different in the arts, and especially in films in which the "author" (director) uses a scenario or a printed novel. Here we find in Freud's mind the same prejudice of "book superiority over film" that I pointed out in Burgess's piece. To the contrary, I consider the "dream work" as a very "creative" activity and the dreamer as a real "director-author" who always uses the techniques of cinema: sequences, overall shots, close-ups, medium-distance views, fade-out, fade-in, dissolves, reverse shots, overhead shots, panning, dolly shots, and the like. There is editing, too, and even stage direction (since people taken out of daily life frequently behave differently in dreams than they do in reality).

Like Monsieur Jourdain's use of "prose" in Molière's play, *Le Bourgeois Gentilhomme*, everyone directs films without being aware of it! The conclusion is inescapable: Everyone can make cinema without any special apprenticeship. The inventions of Edison and the Lumière brothers have simply made it possible for cinema to become "externalized," just as the invention of alphabets made it possible to move from the spoken word to literature.

I believe that because of the kinship of cinema and dreams, film was received enthusiastically and continues to fascinate the public. Technological inventions usually lose their initial cachet after a period of time. Yet today cinema remains as enthralling as it was at its beginning. People were not "bewildered" by the moving images on the silver screen. Right from the start, they accepted its "narrative" so to speak as "natural." Through their dreams, they were already accustomed to cinema's "storytelling" techniques!

Some filmmakers are aware of this kinship, as the following quote from Stanley Kubrick demonstrates:

> I think an audience watching a film is in a state very similar to dreaming, and that the dramatic experience becomes a kind of controlled dream. But the important point here is that the film communicates on a subconscious level, and the audience responds to the basic shape of the story on a subconscious level, as it responds to a dream." (Interview with Bernard Weinraub, *The New York Times*, January 4, 1972)

In a more general way, we can say that dreams use a kind of pictorial or symbolic language that spans the boundaries of cul-

ture and language. This is also the language of "myths." Patrick
Mullahy, a student of Erich Fromm, remarked that "All great
cultures of the past regarded symbolic language and hence
myths and dreams as highly significant and as expressions of
universal and individual experiences; the understanding of symbols became an art which had an important cultural function . . .
This language is one of man's basic modes of expression and we
must understand it if we want to understand ourselves" (*Oedipus: Myth and Complex*, New York, 1948). Symbolic or pictorial
language is therefore a natural gift we humans were born with!

From this vantage point, we can see that both literature (and,
for that matter, all the other arts) and cinema go back to the
beginnings of time. The techniques of cinema, which have always existed at humanity's core, have influenced the most ancient texts and paintings, as we can easily see by analyzing the
Bible and the Arabian Nights or by looking at prehistoric cave
drawings and canvases by Tintoret, Giotto, Raphael, Veronese,
and the like. After all, do we not understand the world through
our senses and primarily through our eyes?

3

Photography, Painting, Cinema, and Realism

From our very beginnings, humankind has tried to conserve images of what we were seeing in the form of drawings, paintings, sculptures, and, later, written descriptions. The invention of photography in 1826 constituted a giant step forward toward that goal. Photography permitted the direct viewing of images of the past; up to that point, that was possible only through paintings and individual memories that invariably altered them. Unlike all other picture making, photography transfers reality from the person, place, or thing to its reproduction. It has a unique, objective quality. It satisfies "once and for all in its very essence, our obsession for realism," wrote André Bazin, the co-founder of *Cahiers du Cinéma*.[7] Bazin, grounded his influential theory of cinema on this objectivity axiom. To him, realism stems more from the means of picture taking than from its product. I, for one, was never at ease with Bazin's view of film's basic realism.

Since childhood, it had struck me that most photographers (including my father, who was an amateur) asked their subjects to look at the camera lens. They lied to kids, telling them that a "birdie" would fly out of it! One day in the 1930s, father, who was on a trip abroad, sent us a photograph of himself at the wheel of a car. But instead of looking at the road, he was staring at the camera! I felt bewildered "How could he drive?" I asked mother "This is a photo," she replied. "One should always turn toward the camera." Things have changed with the development of what is called "art photography." But the trend still endures. Think of the press photos of important people writing at their desks and unrealistically looking at the invisible lens, usually with a smile. At any rate, I forgot my childish astonishment until after World War II when I stumbled on a curious science fiction short story. The title and author's name escape me now. However, it was about a scientist who had invented a camera capable of filming the past. Curious about Newton's adherence to mysticism, the scientist focused his contraption on him. Newton was on his death bed, mumbling, "I knew that He was and still is looking at me!" To Newton, as a character of this story, the camera's lens was god!

People equate the lens with the human eye. The lens looks at us and, therefore, we must look back at it. The lens can also be compared to a vacuum-cleaner, sucking up everything that's photographed. People simply cannot avoid turning toward it! Looking at the camera is, therefore, a perfectly natural reaction.

In movies, things are different because the subjects (actors) are constantly in motion and seldom look at the camera (except when the camera takes the place of one of them!). Moreover, in order to help create a realistic environment the cinematographer tells real people (in the streets) and extras on the sets, not to look at the camera. The lens ceases to resemble a human eye. Rather, it becomes a kind of "pen" with which filmmakers "write" a report (documentaries) or a story (fiction shorts or features). As in photography, the film camera registers images, but it doesn't strive to preserve: Its object is to narrate a fictitious story or a report on some event or travel. In addition, both in photography and cinema, the very presence of the camera and the photographer or the filmmaker necessarily disturbs the matter observed, as modern physics teaches. (Here we touch upon a clear difference between film and literature. The "pen" of the writer cannot be equated with a camera! Indeed, it doesn't register an "ex-

ternal" process but, rather, "translates" an "internal" one. Therefore, it doesn't disturb anything.

For all these reasons, it seems to me difficult to accept the
alleged "innate" realism of the camera. If, as Bazin and Astruc
affirm, the camera doesn't lie, one should also add that it doesn't
necessarily tell the truth. While still in Paris, writing in *Cahiers
du Cinéma*, I had long discussions with Chris Marker, Jean
Rouch, and all the backers of the so-called cinéma verité. Rouch
always claimed for himself the role of a simple instrument, an
extension of the camera, a kind of "living camera," so to speak.
But, in fact, in all Rouch's films there is not a single shot that is
not somehow directed (as in Flaherty's, Vertov's, Ivens's and all
other works of filmmakers who call themselves "documentar-
ists"). *Realism* seems to me a word void of meaning. That probably is one of the reasons why, in the early post-war period, the
expression *neo-realism* was almost spontaneously coined to char-
acterize Rossellini and DeSica's movies. Bazin himself recog-
nized that cinema was not exactly the same as objective reality
but, rather, an asymptote approaching it! I have no intention of
contesting Bazin's writings, which I consider very important and
often illuminating. At any rate, film theory is a relatively recent
discipline and therefore open to discussion. Moreover, recent developments in "cognitive science" seem to indicate that vision
itself is not simply a reflex, a mindless response to light beams
reflected from objects into the retina, but an active process
shaped by the mind. Thus, for instance, Professor Donald D.
Hoffman of the University of California at Irvine says that vision
is not an absolute, but is constructed by the mind (*Visual Intelligence: How We Create What We See*, New York, 1999).

Let me reconstruct at this point a conversation on filmmaking
that I had with Rossellini in an Italian restaurant in Paris (he
adored spaghetti!). He told me about most of the directors I
admired:

> In a way they mislead or, better, they lead the spectator
> with too many "cinematic effects." All these camera move-

ments, trackings, close-ups, special emphasis on important moments. I prefer to remain impassive. What is beautiful in real life is that there is no real or deep difference between momentous events and ordinary ones. They all produce the same impression as the facts of everyday life. I attempt to convey both in the same manner. This method has its own source of dramatic impact. A camera is nothing but a tool. It has a lot of possibilities. I understand young filmmakers who are keen to explore these possibilities. But after a while, one should turn away. I try to minimize my presence as much as possible. You have to let the viewer decide for himself . . . not to dictate your opinions.

True, in retrospect, most of his films seem quite austere!

Today, most photographers claim to be serious artists, creators, authors. I would not deny them such a lofty rank in the realm of Art. Indeed, still pictures, like paintings and drawings, reflect the viewpoint of those who draw or take them. Moreover, they capture a "moment" in the ever-flowing stream of time. While living in Paris, I found in the flea market a nineteenth century or early twentieth century picture of a group of people playing croquet on the lawn of an English country estate, with some guests watching them or resting in the sun. The way they looked at one another fascinated me and suggested a lot of thoughts about their relationships. I envisioned writing a novel that would simply describe the still picture and let readers infer for themselves a drama out of the objective description. The ultimate objective novel! But my first drafts were rather subjective and I abandoned my project. This exercise convinced me that, even in still photographs, there exists an insurmountable abyss between images and words.

Coming back to the question of photography's authorship, I think that every picture contains the photographer's imprint inasmuch as her vision is delineated by the rectangle or the square of her camera and that she chooses to frame in it an event or people from a certain angle. Let's consider, for instance, a newspaper photo showing a meeting between two heads of state.

There is not only a meeting going on between the two men in the picture, but also between them and the photographer. True, if the photographer had not been there at the right time, the meeting, as a historic event, would have still taken place, but without its public display in the paper. The image registered by the photographer adds another dimension to the event.

Both photography and cinema use images as a mode of expression. Nevertheless, the image on a film, as opposed to the image in a photo, has no meaning whatsoever. The message of a film resides in the concatenation of its images!

As for paintings, some of the great canvases do suggest the idea of movement. They become "animated" in the eyes of the beholder. A few years back, in a book called *Moving Pictures*,[8] Anne Hollander contended that much of European painting was predicated on a way of ordering the visual world that would now be called *cinematic*, with an implication that something was happening beyond the picture frame. She also remarked that cinema, for its part, "composes" images (using light and dark, color, tone, and hue) in patterns already explored and set by great painters of the past. In her opinion, artists like Goya and Turner "struggled to make the single picture do what film has done since. . . . The story, whatever it is, is not told in 'pictures' . . . it is brought to life as if it were happening, not being told at all."

The Mexican diplomat, novelist, and essayist Carlos Fuentes made a similar remark about Velazquez's portrait of *Las Meninas*. While visiting Madrid's Prado Museum, he was struck by the movement spectators discern in this painting. The novelist Philip Roth, who accompanied him, underscored the "narrative possibilities" contained in the canvas.[9] Let me quote here a few lines from the article Fuentes published about his experience:

> The painter is facing the very canvas that we are seeing. He is painting as he sees us. Everyone in the painting . . . is looking out. The French philosopher Michel Foucault answered the question, What are they looking at? by reminding us that in a mirror at the back of the canvas, the

infanta's parents, King Philip and Queen Mariana, are reflected. . . . The painting looks at us; we look at the painting
and, as the essayist and philosopher Ortega Y. Gasset observed in his study of Velazquez, a double dynamic is established: We are invited into the painting, but we also
invite the painting out of itself toward us. The painting
exists because we see it, do we, too, exist because the painting sees us?

The answer to this question lies in the realm of metaphysics. As
for Fuentes's remark that the painting exists because we see it,
this is somehow obvious: Beauty (art) exists in the eye of the
beholder! At any rate, a friend of mine (the French painter Pierre
Lesieur) used to say that some paintings are mute and others
speak; a few invite us to enter into them!

Velazquez's *Las Meninas* reminds me of movies in which the
director is himself in the cast and sometimes seems to be looking
at the audience from the silver screen! Hitchcock always made
a cameo appearance in his movies, even in *Lifeboat*, in which the
limited space of the small vessel did not allow him to do so. Yet
he managed to put in the hands of one of the protagonists a
newspaper with his photo on the front page.

Coming back to Fuentes's essay on Velazquez, I really don't
see his point, all artists are present in their work and look at the
spectator from their own vantage point. They don't need to paint
themselves or to play a part. Indeed, Renoir and Matisse, to
name just two, are in all their canvases. In the realm of cinema,
then, the author (the director) is "hidden" in his mise-en-scène.

Actually, the affinity between painting and cinema should not
surprise us; after all, painters as well as writers and, later on,
photographers and filmmakers, are all unconsciously inspired by
the "moving images" of their nightly dream productions! They
all strive to recreate "images in movement," each through his
own medium. Indeed, people have always yearned for images.
Hence, the drawings in prehistoric caves and the painted "cur-
tains" itinerant storytellers of the Orient unfolded before their

audiences to complement certain episodes of their oral stories. Hence, too, the illustrations in ancient manuscripts. For instance, Persian and Indian miniatures were designed to highlight written texts, not to hang on walls! (In the same vein, stained glass windows and murals in churches were not ornaments but "messages" to the believers.)

Book authors and booksellers had often considered illustrations a powerful means of clarifying the meaning of written texts and of promoting their sale. Thus, long before the invention of cinema there had been attempts at "translating" words into images.

This practice, which still exists in modern publishing, especially in the realm of children's books, has nurtured misunderstandings concerning the relations of printed words and cinema. Some experts go as far as to consider motion pictures simple illustrations of a written text, book or script.

4

Influence of Literature on Cinema

In a well-known essay, titled "Dickens, Griffith and Us," the famous Russian director Serguei Eisenstein argues that in his style of storytelling as well as in his vision of the characters and their environment, Dickens used many of the basic elements and tools of cinema. Eisenstein gives many examples of Dicken's use of quick cuts, close-ups, split-screen, and the like. He also shows that Griffith used Dicken's narrative methods in his films.

Indeed, the manner in which D. W. Griffith tells a story parallels that of the author of *Great Expectations*. The American filmmaker's widow reported the following telling incident: In the scene in *Enoch Arden* in which Enoch's wife is waiting for his return, Griffith shows only a close-up of her face immediately after cutting away from Enoch, lost on a desert island. His producer protested: "How can you tell a story with such sudden jumps? Nobody will understand." Griffith retorted, "Didn't Dickens write this way?" The producer replied, "Yes. But that was Dickens. He was writing novels. It is completely different." Griffith retorted, "The difference is not so great: I am making novels with images!"

But is this not the road to tautology? It seems to me that Eisenstein and everyone else who sought to link cinema to literature went to a great deal of trouble to state the obvious. Since the invention of alphabets, writers used the innate dream's mechanisms to tell stories. Over the centuries and millennia, they perfected these "narrative techniques" in their literary medium. I don't know if they were aware of the influence of dreams on their work.

Yet, curiously enough, in the second half of the nineteenth century, Nathaniel Hawthorne considered writing a novel that would mirror our dreams, with all the incoherences and oddnesses of our sleeping visions. He wondered why nobody had undertaken such a literary venture before. He himself never finished his project, but it is remarkable for a "pre-cinema" writer to have related dreams to novels. In the first decades of the twentieth century, James Joyce and some surrealists actually carried out Hawthorne's idea!

Almost at the same time as Hawthorne, the French poet Baudelaire wrote the following verses:

> Étonnants voyageurs, quelles nobles histoires
> Nous lisons dans vos yeux, profonds comme des
>   mers!
> Ouvrez-nous les écrins de vos riches mémoires,
> Les bijoux merveilleux faits d'astres et d'ethers.
> Nous voulons voyager sans vapeur et sans voile.
> Faites, pour égayer l'ennui de nos prisons.
> Passer sur nos esprits tendus comme une toile
> Vos souvenirs, avec leurs cadres d'horizons?
>   ("Voyages")

Was he prefiguring the silver screen and travelogues? Consider, too, this curious entry in Swift's *Journal to Stella* (March 27, 1713): "I went afterward to see a famous moving picture (*sic*) and I never saw anything so pretty. You see a sea ten inches wide, a town at the other end, and ships sailing in the sea and discharging their cannon." Did Swift momentarily cross into a parallel universe in which cinema had already been invented?

Carlos Fuentes once remarked:

Denis Diderot, the great spirit of the French eighteenth century, asked a novel not only to narrate, but also to move.
Do not describe, he begs, go to the fact. I meet a woman
as beautiful as an angel. I want to go to bed with her; I go,
I have four children." Diderot in a way, filmed his own
novels: He does not have to describe what we see; instead
he edits his words, cuts away, flashes back and forth.[10]

In the mid-1980s, Italo Calvino, a major twentieth century Italian writer and essayist, affirmed that the imagination uses two
methods—one starts with spoken words that merge into visual
images; the other starts with visual images that work their way
toward verbal expression. Reading exemplifies the first method.
Reading a novel or a news item in a paper prompts us to visualize, more or less successfully, the reported events. Cinema exemplifies the second method. The image on the screen has passed
through a written text (script); the director has visualized it mentally and then materially reconstructed it on the set before filming it. Therefore, every film is the outcome of a series of material
and non-material operations during which the images take form.
In this process, the imagination's *mental cinema* plays as important a part as that of the actual filming and editing. This mental
cinema continually operates in everyone; it has always operated
even before the invention of cinema; it never ceases to project
images on our *internal screen*.[11] Oddly enough, Calvino did not
specifically refer to dreams in his essay. His remarks were intended for the 1985–86 Charles Eliot Norton lectures at Harvard
University, but a stroke killed him that same fall. The unrevised
text was published without any editing in 1988 in a volume titled
Lezioni Americane: Sei proposte per il prossimo millennio. In the
fourth lecture, titled "Visibility," from which I have extracted the
above remarks, Calvino insisted on what he called the "priority
of the visual image."

At any rate, the camera, invented at the end of the nineteenth
century, fell in the hands of people brought up on literary culture. Naturally, early filmmakers could turn for inspiration only

to the novelists and dramatists, unaware that they were actually digging in their own in-born dream experience. Moreover, a whole literary genre indirectly mimicked dreams (especially nightmares) in their content (but not in their discontinuous manner, as Hawthorne had suggested). Fantasy and horror novels are as old as literature itself and continue to appeal to large audiences; the same can be said of "gothic" stories. This can be considered the first direct influence of "cinema" on literature!

It is no secret that cinema draws inspiration from literature: The immense number of adaptations clearly speaks for itself! Cinema and literature also share a number of technical devices. But these are basic narrative techniques, not methods peculiar to the two arts. In fact, cinema and literature use very different materials: Words, even when they succeed in creating "visual" impressions, are never images. The novelist seeks to translate his view with words, just as the filmmaker does with images. Besides, the techniques of the dream predated both literature and cinema.

Film's impact on literature is equally clear. References to cinema abound in writing. For instance, in the early 1960s, when the "Old Vic" presented its Shakespearian repertoire at the Theatre des Nations in Paris, the French novelist Elsa Triolet titled her review "Hamlet the James Dean of Year 1600" ("Les Lettres Françaises," June 6, 1962). In fact, the influence of film on literature has been much more profound than literature's impact on film. When cinema took over narrative techniques, it compelled literature to seek new paths, just as photography changed paintings. This all the more so because film extended its shoots in all directions. While *The Godfather* or *In The Line of Fire* tell a linear story in the manner of the traditional novel, the cinematic techniques of narrative have become highly diversified and complicated. There is no longer a story in the classical sense in Welles's *M. Arkadin* or in Godard's films. The new forms of storytelling have multiplied: Journalistic investigation (*Citizen Kane*), anthropological study (Rouch's *Moi un Noir*), political examination (Costa-Gavras's *Z*), apocalyptic parable (Kubrick's *Dr. Strange-*

love), phantasmagoric ballet (Fellini's *Giulieta Degli Spiriti*), historical essay (Rossellini's *La Prise du Pouvoir Par Louis XIV*), self-analysis (Ingmar Bergman's *Wild Strawberries*), and so forth.

In an essay, titled "Quick Cuts: The Novel Follows Film into a World of Fewer Words," E. L. Doctorow noted:

> The effect of a hundred years of filmmaking on the practice of literature has been considerable. The twentieth century novel minimizes discourse that dwells on settings, characters' CVs and the like. The writer finds it preferable to incorporate all necessary information in the action, to carry it along in the current of the narrative, as is done in movies.[12]

Doctorow also cited the influence of filmic "cut," which instantly repositions the scenes in space and time and allows "daring uses of discontinuity that have occurred from violations of the grammatical protocols of person or tense."

I remember a piece by Tom McDonough, a cameraman-writer, titled "That Great Blank Page, the Screen," published in the *New York Times Book Review* (November 15, 1987). He wrote, "They say I am cinematic. Since I make most of my living as a cinematographer, it would appear that when I write, I do so under the influence of movies." He quoted at one point the following remark by Whitney Balliet: "Novels were once panoramas, chronicles, labyrinths, whole subcontinents, but movies have taken over these comprehensive tasks, and the novel has been increasingly made out of glimpses, incidents, small happenings."

In Europe and, more particularly, in France, a literary school in the 1960s, called the "Nouveau Roman" (New Novel) tried to renovate literature and transform novels into a kind of "film (or images) made with words." The general idea was to *describe* events and characters as *objectively* as possible and let the reader become a sort of *viewer*. Later on, I shall return to this attempt by novelists to capture the essence of cinema.

5

Some Misunderstandings

For the time being, I would like to dwell on some other misunderstandings affecting the relationship between literature and
cinema. One of the most current could be called the *easy grasp of
image*. It is assumed *a priori* that it is easier to watch a film than
to read a book. That might be true of a simple linear story (such
as in some of the early westerns or short (two reels) slapstick
comedies, which were understood by illiterate audiences all over
the world. But it is certainly not true of complicated tragedies
or whodunits. Let me cite here a personal experience that gives
the lie to the ingrained belief of the easiness of cinema. During
the 1960s, the World Health Organization (WHO) sponsored a
film intended to persuade people in Africa to accept vaccinations
against infectious diseases. The script could not have been simpler. First, the patient's parents summoned the local medicine-
man (shaman) to their hut. The patient was growing worse by
the hour. Then came the WHO doctor, who saved the patient
with a shot. The film was shown in a village and the supervising
official asked the audience to describe what they had seen. For
a while, no one spoke. Finally one man said, "I saw a hen going
into the hut." In fact, while the film was being shot, a hen *had*
entered the hut at the most dramatic moment, but the director,

who was satisfied with his scene, did not want to shoot it over lest the characters be unable to act as well in a second take. In the case of another WHO film about malaria shown in an Asian village, the audience refused to take the medicine on the grounds that they did not have "giant" mosquitoes in their environment. Indeed the film contained many enlargements of the insects! Understanding the images depends on many conventions, which differ according to the cultural background of the spectators. Images certainly do not have the same "meaning" everywhere!

This myth of the easy grasp of image has been crossed with the myth of the image offering a more precise view than the written description. However hard writers try, they can never totally convey in words their *impression* (vision) of a table, whereas a photograph of a film transmits instantaneously all there is to know visually about the same table and its surroundings. Everybody knows the saying "A picture is worth a thousand words." We were always told that it stemmed from Chinese wisdom. In fact, that slogan was invented in the 1920s by an American advertiser named Fred R. Barnard.[13] Whatever its origin, it certainly contains a measure of truth. The Franco-American novelist and academician Julien Green expressed it in his own way: "It is somehow naïve to try at all costs to convey with words the curve and rosiness of a cheek, the color of eyes, the exasperating mystery of a glance."[14]

At first glance, this seems obvious. But is it? If it were really so, why is it that the cinema is used less than the printed word for purposes of communication? Here we have to draw a line between photography and cinema Photos are "still": We can take time to examine them and study their details. They might represent hundreds of pages of written text. Film images, on the other hand, are elusive and projected in rapid sequence on the silver screen. In actuality, film expression and its grasp by the spectator are often much more difficult than literary expression and reading, if only because the visual includes too much. In a certain way, film resembles a "cybernetic" machine. It retransmits by way of the screen a great number of simultaneous messages (information that comes from the setting, the costumes, the lighting, the actors' gestures and changes of place, the camera's movements, the lines spoken, the sound effects, etc.) Add to these the cutting, the editing, the length and character of shots and sequences, and the like. (The particular way in which each filmmaker employs these various elements constitutes the very essence of her "direction," "style," what we called mise-en-scène, for want of a better word, in the 1950s in *Cahiers du Cinéma*). So there is, in effect, a *poliphony of information* in film in contrast to the *monody* of literature.

In the same order of ideas, it is inaccurate to speak of cinema as a "universal language." Indeed, there are as many ways of expressing oneself through moving images as there are filmmakers and countries. To be convinced of this, we need only view in succession films by Kenjo Mizogushi, Jean Renoir, John Ford, Satjyatit Ray, Ingmar Bergman, Martin Scorcese, Woody Allen, Abbas Kiarostami, Steven Spielberg, and Roberto Benigni. They all use the cinematographic image in different ways! Though westerns seem to find audiences everywhere, in contrast to the work of a Fellini or a Buñuel, this is probably because they express basic, simple, unsophisticated feelings and because they tell stories with ups and downs and reversals that correspond to the saga of all humanity. Most spectators look at the "story" (the "subject") not at the "film"; or at what the "author" wants to convey, or at his "style." (The real film fan, the "connoisseur," by contrast, is interested in the "style," i.e., what in the film does not merge with the subject!) Most spectators are not concerned about the author's "universe"; they do not care whether Visconti or Coppola's signature is on the movie. They have not progressed beyond the "genres": They go to see comedies, crime stories, dramas, mysteries, horror pictures, and the like. They go to see Tom Cruise, Julia Roberts, Demi Moore, Mel Gibson, or Denzel Washington. They are attracted by stars, not by meanings.

On the other hand, the "specialists" who profess to be interested solely in the "author" and not in the story (scenario),

evince a kind of "reverse" prejudice, born of snobbery. One has
only to go to "film libraries" or "art theaters" to see them chuck-
ling smugly and flaunting their "superiority" with every gab-
bling Japanese or Chinese (and now Iranian!) film shown
without subtitles. As if speech could be divorced from image in
talkies. Even the silent films included some dialogue in the form
of interspersed captions.

In short, looking at a film is not necessarily easier than reading
a book. The only thing that makes cinema easier is that it does
not require years of studying grammar and vocabulary! Spectators can walk into the theater and enjoy (or dislike) the movie,
they need no special preparation. As I have made reference to
spectators, let me cite another misunderstanding, which has to
do with the notion of "audience." For many people, cinema is a
"mass art," intended for wide audiences, while literature is con-
sumed by a numerically more limited "elite." Cinema is *sheer
entertainment*, proclaim some members of the literary establishment and, save for a few exceptions, films lower the level of
taste. A decade or so ago, a distinguished professor of English,
Jerome Charyn, published a book called *Movieland: Hollywood and
the Great American Dream Culture*, in which he wrote: "I can say
without melodrama or malice that Hollywood ruined my life. In
his opinion, films keep viewers in "a state of constant adolescence." Like the ghostly shadows of Plato's cave, the screen images alienate us further from ourselves! At about the same time,
Guy Debord, a French sociologist, contended that with the in-
vading entertainment, images are replacing real life, anesthetiz-
ing the public ("Commentaires Sur la Société du Spectacle,"
1988). Such gloomy views are not new. Nor are they limited to
cinema. They appear often in the form of articles, books, talk
shows, even congressional inquiries and debates. They espouse
more or less radical condemnations. As an example, consider a
1985 book condemning television without appeal! It was written
by Neil Postman, a professor of communications at New York
University under a telling title: *Amusing Ourselves to Death: Public
Discourse in the Age of Show Business*. Referring to Aldous Hux-

ley's *Brave New World* and George Orwell's *Nineteen Eighty-Four*, he upheld the former's view that our "decline and decadence" would come disguised under the garb of entertainment. In Postman's opinion, television has already altered public discourse by making entertainment the format for presentation of all experience; in short, apocalypse now!

To such an argument I would retort: "So what?" Doesn't entertainment satisfy some of our vital needs? Without it, humans would rapidly wither away. After all what is "escapism," if not the power and product of imagination? Half a century ago, Johan Huizinga, in his celebrated *Homo Ludens*, argued that play was the central element in human culture. And some years later the philosopher Joseph Pieper published *Leisure: The Basis of Culture*! Returning to movies, I would say that a really entertaining movie cannot harm the viewer. Good movies are entertaining! In 1997, *Contact* pretended to be a movie for grown-ups. It illustrated the tensions between science and religion, reason and faith. It asked "big" questions: Are we alone in the universe? Can science and religion co-exist? A budget of $90 million was spent. The movie was a bore! Yet Robert Zemeckis had previously directed *Forrest Gump*, which was entertaining *and* contained a hidden "meaning"!

I would finally ask: What is Art's purpose if not entertainment of the public? As André Malraux once remarked, photography has made out of "art" an "entertainment" accessible to millions upon millions of people. Great paintings, music, beautiful landscapes, extraordinary stories—all of that is meant to delight people, to entertain them. The need for entertainment is inscribed in our genes. I consider that dreams constitute the entertainment of our sleep time! Nights without dream would become unbearable! Shaharazad's royal husband probably suffered from some sort of inability to dream. Thanks to his "malady," humanity gained an immortal masterpiece, "The Thousand and One Nights"! Shaharazad was a "living television set" and at the same time the producer of a "late show"!

In addition, the critics of mass culture and sheer entertainment

ignore the huge success of crime fiction and the remarkable con-
sumption of comic strips and books in many countries. While
the literary establishment does not consider detective stories as
part of literature, their disdain has been shattered in the second
half of the twentieth century: Dashiell Hammett, Raymond
Chandler, John LeCarré, and other "crime" writers have entered
the realm of "high" literature. In any case, cinema has erased
such a distinction: Some film masterpieces are detective stories,
and we demonstrated in the 1950s and 1960s in the *Cahiers du
Cinéma* that Hitchcock movies, for instance, were as meaningful
and artistic as the best works of literature.

Still, the prejudice against film remains and producers think
they are giving the public what it wants. But their definition of
the public is oddly vague. Occasionally it narrows down enough
to include such concepts as "the man on the street" or the "average spectator." Behind these concepts looms large a desire to
reduce all of humanity to a "single essence." This reminds me
of Genghis Khan, who dreamed of a world having a single head
to be cut off with a single saber slash!

Finally, a few additional words about realism in cinema. I have
already mentioned André Bazin's theory of the photo and film
camera's "innate" realism. Let me observe that the camera and
projector inventors, the brothers Lumière, never imagined that
their contraption could be anything else than an instrument for
reproducing the real world But does it? Without color and sound?
Moreover, are cutting, montage, fade-ins, close-ups, and many
other techniques used in films merely *reflecting* reality? And what
about the positioning of the camera in a particular spot? And
the start and stoppage of filming at a particular moment? And
the projection on a flat surface? Indeed, a deep gap separates the
"representation" from the "real." In their own way, films are as
"unrealistic" as novels. They reflect the point of view of the filmmaker.

In any case, the old belief that "the camera never lies" has
become meaningless in our age of technological leaps. Films such

as *Forrest Gump* and *Terminator 2*, to mention only two titles among a rapidly growing list of new productions, underscore the fact that any image can be (and actually is) manipulated, combined, or morphed into anything else! What is "reality" in such a new technological environment? And what is realism?

It is said that the spectators of the first Lumière show in the basement of the Café de la Paix in Paris were frightened by the entry of the train's engine in La Ciotat station and rushed toward the exits. I would believe it. But it was not because of the "realism" of the moving pictures that they were frightened. It was rather because it reminded them of their own nightmares (black and white, aggrandized images). Cinema's relationship to reality is not very different from its relationship to dreams! Realism in cinema is nothing but a style of narration. As physicists well know, the observer influences the matter observed. Films cannot be more realistic or objective than books and literature! Moreover, we should not forget that both cinema and literature are essentially entertainment, not means of mirroring the so-called "real" world. As Gore Vidal once wrote: "Visual images are so powerful that we are both defined and manipulated by fictions of such potency that they are able to replace our own experience" (*Screening History*, Harvard University, 1992).

These are some of the misunderstandings that have marked the relationship between film and literature I think that the preceding inventory has helped to clarify the differences between them, at least enough to clear the way to see the essential: an examination of the two modes of expression in their specificity. For the rest of the discussion, I will try to restrict myself more particularly to the common denominator of both domains, which is narration. What, from this point of view, distinguishes the two arts?

6

Film Shows, Literature Says

At first blush, film "shows" and literature "says." Readers do not "see" what they are being told. They read words that refer them to someone else's (real or imaginary) "lived" experience. They personally compose in their mind more or less accurate images after reading the printed words. In a way, they *illustrate what they are reading*; they transform it into a kind of "film" that they project, as it were, on the screen of their own imaginations. Images are therefore essential both in cinema and literature (indeed as previously indicated, ancient manuscripts were often illustrated!).

Until a relatively recent period, novels were based on a kind of "judgment" made by their authors on a certain "reality" that they proposed to depict. With writers like Flaubert, for instance, the novel ceased to look toward "judgments" and turned instead to "facts." Maupassant, in his own words, wanted to *"cause to pass before our eyes"* both characters and events. The novel was already seeking to become so to speak, "viewable!" With the invention of the film camera and projector, this "longing" heated up. Dos Passos's *Manhattan Transfer* and the French "Nouveau Roman" of the '50s and '60s, with their pretensions to *objectivity*, are, in a certain sense, the outcome of this pre-cinema "desire to become viewable." In this respect, Alain Robbe-Grillet's work is exemplary. He himself wrote in an essay: "To describe things is to place oneself deliberately outside them, confronting them. It is a matter of no longer appropriating them to oneself or of carrying anything over to them. To confine oneself to description is obviously to reject all other ways of approaching objects: Sympathy as unrealistic, tragedy as alienating, comprehension as deriving solely from the domain of science. Sight immediately emerges as the privileged sense from this point of view" (*La Nouvelle Revue Française*, June 1954). The "novel of *sight*," as these works were dubbed, endeavours to rid itself of all meanings of the novel of the past, in order to confront us with things and persons as they are, here and now. Previously, the novel was the epitome of the "art of the past" (in the sense that its events had already come into existence before the writing and the reading). The "nouveau roman" is written in the present tense and professes to restrict itself to showing the spectacle of things.

In this respect, Robbe-Grillet's *La Jalousie* is a typical example: Reduced to being a mere observer, its central character, a jealous husband, never appears, even in the form of a narrating *I*, only his unvaryingly immediate vision is presented to the reader. In this connection it is worth recalling Robert Montgomery's 1946 film *Lady in the Lake*, based entirely on the protagonist's point of view; the camera takes the "first-person" point of view of Detective Philip Marlowe; we see his face only once, in a mirror. This kind of film is called *subjective* in contrast to the novel of the same style, which is dubbed *objective!* Furthermore, this technique is often employed by filmmakers to concentrate on what the protagonist sees. A well-known instance is the long sequence of the doctor's arrival at his fiancée's house in Rouben Mamoulian's *Dr. Jekyll and Mr. Hyde* (1932).

In support of his thesis, Robbe-Grillet cited as a model of objective representation the "filmed" chair as opposed to the chair described in a book. For one thing, it is there before our eyes in a visibility impervious to all interrelation; for another, its appearance takes place now, in the present.

At any rate, it is evident that the efforts of the Nouveau Roman are linked to the dissemination and prestige of the modes of visual transmission in the contemporary world. Almost from its beginnings in the early years of the twentieth century, the cinema taught the novel speed, elimination of smugness, and abandonment of endless commentaries. Not all writers got the message. As the great French author, Louis-Ferdinand Céline, said in 1954 in an "imaginary" interview he wrote himself: "It seems that today's novelists are not yet aware of the existence of cinema and of the fact that cinema has rendered useless and even ridiculous their way of writing. Their novels are nothing more than commercial scripts waiting for a filmmaker."[15]

In a way, the Nouveau Roman recalls the Camera-Eye movement initiated by the Russian documentary producer Dziga Vertov in the '30s and developed in the '60s by such directors as Jean Rouch and Chris Marker under the name cinéma-vérité. The long contemplation of a doorknob, a window, or a road sign in Robbe-Grillet's books, reminds us that cinema lingered over such things before it had attained to the use of words. The Nouveau Roman's fixation on such details points out that it adopted visual techniques of the '20s that filmmakers were striving to rid themselves of. It makes me wonder whether the authors of the Nouveau Roman were not obsessed with a haunting nostalgia for the silent movies.

Yet one cannot help underlining a basic contradiction in Robbe-Grillet's literary endeavor. Formal description is never image, and the chair "reported" by the "eye" will never coincide with the "filmed" chair. In *Lady in the Lake* we see what the protagonist sees. In *La Jalousie*, we read a report of what the husband sees. Here we touch upon an *irreducible* difference—at least in the present state of technology—between film and literature, a difference that for years has fueled endless arguments on the "fidelity" of adaptations of great novels. To me the very idea of fidelity is somehow oxymoronic: One author cannot take another's place, unless she wants to court a plagiarism lawsuit! And to come back to Anthony Burgess's article, quoted earlier.

I would say that when we see *A Clockwork Orange* we are dealing with a film by Kubrick, not with Burgess's book! Both in its content and its style, it reflects Kubrick's preoccupations and style, which we know from having seen his earlier films.

7

The Question of Adaptations

The movie *A Clockwork Orange* is a Kubrick *film*, not a Burgess *book*. And it could not be otherwise. Even when the scriptwriter is the author of the adapted book, the film remains the creative product of its director! Indeed, the latter cannot become the book's author. He cannot "feel" like the author. He cannot have exactly the same interests and tastes. He cannot share exactly the same viewpoint. He cannot look at the world and the characters in the same way. In order to avoid generalizations, let us choose an example. Let us, for instance, consider Tolstoy's *Anna Karenina*, which was adapted for the screen several times—by Clarence Brown in 1932 (Greta Garbo, Frederic March); by Julien Duvivier in 1948 (Vivien Leigh, Ralph Richardson); by Alexandre Zarkhi in 1965 (Tatiana Samoilova); by Simon Langton (for television) in 1985 (Jacqueline Bisset, Christopher Reeve).

The first thing that strikes one is that these films are completely different from one another. They also are different from *my* impression of the book. Yet they all tell the same story, an account of the love affair between a married woman and an officer of the Russian army. By itself, this story synopsis reveals neither the real nature of the book nor the talent of its author. The "genius" of Tolstoy, the real "meaning" of his novel, is not in the story he relates. It lies in *the part of his book that does not coincide with the plot.* After all, Anna's story is a commonplace adultery, a pedestrian affair. The book presents a fresco of a decaying society and a description of several schemes and affairs that intersect at last. The novel starts with Anna's brother's marriage in turmoil and a projected wedding that does not take place. Anna comes to town to "save" her brother's household and instead becomes involved in events that destroy her own conjugal ties. All these troubles precipitate Anna's distress and solitude. Continuous movement from the countryside to the city and vice versa punctuate the events. And, last but not least, the characters, in turn, reflect the contradictions of their society. The core of *Anna Karenina* does not lie in the story of a troubled married woman, but in the way Tolstoy uses that story to express himself. The great Russian author could have borrowed Flaubert's famous phrase and said: "I am Anna Karenina!" ("Mme. Bovary, c'est moi!")

A curious incident reported by Hermann Hesse in his *Autobiographical Writings* will perhaps further clarify the foregoing. During a cure in Baden, an angry reader criticized one of his novels scathingly. Hesse responded: "My book, like any poetic creation, did not consist merely of content but rather the content was relatively unimportant, just as unimportant as the possible intentions of the author. The important thing for us artists was whether, as a result of the intentions, meaning, and thoughts of the author, a pattern woven of language stuff, of language yarn, emerged whose immeasurable worth stood far above the measurable worth of the content. [The reader] was speaking, to be sure, simply of the content. The rest had not touched him." This is exactly what we tried to explain about films in the *Cahiers du Cinéma.* This is what we called mise-en-scène, or style. As Carl Dreyer, the great Danish filmmaker of yore, used to say: "The soul of a movie appears in its style." Most of the viewers, including many critics, usually remain on the level of "content" (i.e., the story), ignoring the rest—what does not "coincide" with the story!

To come back to Tolstoy, we see that the novel *Anna Karenina* is a succession of imagined scenes that reverberate and have been carefully *coordinated* by the author. Through this coordination, Tolstoy has imposed a *structure* that is unique and in which he has insuflated life. This gives to the novel a distinctive character that reflects its *style* a particular *form* that contains the *hidden meaning* of the work. This *form* and this *meaning* are Tolstoy's alone. Nobody else can reproduce them. Imitations only pale by comparison to the original. No adaptation can reproduce that part of Tolstoy's creation. No script can capture his personal genius.

Therefore, right from the start of scriptwriting, Tolstoy is excluded from the adaptation. The filmmakers have just borrowed Anna Karenina's story. To respond to the imperatives of the medium, they have left out a number of the subplots, schematizing the story. But, like Tolstoy himself, they do not want to limit their filming to the story alone. Therefore, they try to create their own overall *structure*, their own perspective and meaning, their own coordination of the scenes. They do their best to take advantage of the talent of the actors, the cinematographer, the other professionals involved in the production. The end-product we see on the silver screen is *their work, not that of Tolstoy*. Of the four adaptations I cited above, the first—the one by Clarence Brown—is, in my opinion, the best. It has nothing to do with Tolstoy's novel, but it stands well, on its own!

As a kid, I used to think that I knew Hugo's *Les Miserables*, having seen the film made by the French director Raymond Bernard (1933) with the bulky Harry Baur playing Jean Valjean. A couple of years later I saw the American version (Richard Boleslawski, 1935) with a slim and elegant Frederic March in Valjean's part. I was amazed by the enormous differences between the two films and especially between the two actors. Finally, when I read the book, I understood that the films had just simplified the plot and reduced the number of characters as well as episodes. I also realized another basic difference between literature and cinema. Indeed, films impose a "figuration" of the characters while in a novel it is up to readers to build up their own "image" of the characters. The reverse is sometimes true. Thus, I continue to imagine Anna Karenina looking like Greta Garbo and Jean Valjean resembling Harry Baur!

Novelists are wrong to get angry at such things, especially those who have been paid enormous amounts of money for the use of their stories. As for the borrowing of titles of great books of the past, this is a commercial question that has to do with the producers and distributors. In any case, the film is not the reflection of the book and, hence, can neither betray nor transcend it. It is a new work that has a different author and, in the case of the movie *A Clockwork Orange*, with all due respect to Burgess, the author is the director—Kubrick! As Kubrick explained at the time the movie was released, "The film itself is a merciless vision of the near-future. Roving gangs rape, kill, maim and steal. Citizens live in a vandalized pop art culture, gaudy, icy and filthy. Politicians and the police are vicious" (*New York Times*, January 4, 1972). The so-called New Wave of the '50s in France (at the time when it restricted itself to film criticism), had the good sense to follow Truffaut's distinction between great directors who were real "authors" of their movies and those who were content to "illustrate" a script. Hitchcock, Hawks, Rossellini, Buñuel, Mizoguchi, Coppola, Scorcese, and some others are as much *authors* as Burgess (perhaps even more so).

I would feel remiss if I did not mention André Bazin's ideas about adaptations. He distinguished three periods in the history of cinema. In its first years, the producers selected established works—mainly well-known novels—while testing the boundaries of the new technology. Between the two world wars, they translated literary work after literary work into the new medium. This was the era of dominance of form over content. The post-1945 era, Bazin said, can be called "the era of the scenario." As Dudley Andrew wrote in his book on Bazin: "Now certain filmmakers could think of filming a novel in a way which would preserve that novel's uniqueness, and adaptation could become a way of re-experiencing a cultural object not *as cinema* but *through it*."[16] Bazin chose as an example Robert Bresson's adaptation of Bernanos's *Diary of a Country Priest*, in which the film-maker avoided "easy capitulations to cinema." Bresson, Bazin said, followed the novel phrase by phrase: "It is not a question of being faithful to the original because, to begin with, it *is* the novel."[17] According to Bazin, novels are cultural artifacts that can be converted into cinema like any other artifact. Bresson filmed *Diary* like a documentary director, while David Lean "regularized" Pasternak's *Dr. Zhivago* until the latter obeyed the laws and look of cinema. I beg to disagree with my late friend and editor of the *Cahiers du Cinéma*. Film can never be a book and vice versa. No matter how close Bresson's vision is to that of Bernanos, the two artists nevertheless differ. *Diary of a Country Priest* reflects Bresson's "world," not that of Bernanos! It is true that Bresson tried very hard to follow the book page by page. However, he could not reproduce Bernanos's vision, at best, he conveyed to the audience what he (Bresson) thought was Bernanos's vision!

In January 1954, *Cahiers du Cinéma* published a vitriolic attack by François Truffaut against a famous French scriptwriter and the top directors for whom he worked. The scriptwriter, Jean Aurenche, had asserted that scenes in novels were either "cinematic" or "non-cinematic." For the latter, he would create "cinematic equivalent" ones. Truffaut was appalled by Aurenche's arrogance; he accused Aurenche of *betraying* the great French novelists and trying to "rewrite" important works of literature. In our discussions, I noted that his famous 1954 article seemed to contradict his theory of directors' "authorship." He pointed out that the "story" is not at the heart of either films or novels! Moreover, no scriptwriter or film director can convey the gist of the great novels. Truffaut was a "fighter." He himself changed many things in the books he adapted for the screen! For instance, he drastically reduced the number of Jeanne Moreau's lovers in *Jules et Jim*! As time passed, he modified many of his previous "critical" opinions.

Jean Cocteau who saw *Gone with the Wind* in December 1944 at a private screening at the American Embassy in Paris, noted in his diary (December 3, 1944) that the screen adaptation had followed the book "to the letter." The historic events (war scenes) were wonderfully rendered while the "psychological scenes" were flat because that part of the book was itself mediocre! He concluded that the "book" should have been rewritten for the screen! He probably ignored the fact that the film had had several directors! It was not an auteur movie!

8

Cinema and Theater

The motion picture industry not only turns to novels, but it also uses plays. For that reason, when speaking of adaptations, André Bazin included in his text considerations about the relationship between cinema and theater. In his opinion, theater, as opposed to film, is characterized by the *artificiality* of its dramatic and scenic design. While adapting a play, cinema should restrict itself to this artificiality instead of turning it into a screenplay; the human voice, which is the dominant medium of theatrical art, would be weakened or even lost in adaptations unless the filmmaker curbed cinema's *expansiveness*. Cinema better serves both itself and theater by emphasizing the sparseness and compactness that, in Bazin's words, make plays "the drama of the wills of men against men or men against God." Bazin gave as examples of good cinematic adaptations, Laurence Olivier in *Henry V* (1944), Orson Welles in *Macbeth* (1948), Jean Cocteau in *Les Parents Terribles* (1948), and William Wyler in *The Little Foxes* (1941). He wrote, "There is a hundred times more cinema, and better cinema at that, in one fixed shot in *The Little Foxes* or *Macbeth* than in all the exterior traveling shots, in all the natural settings . . . by means of which up to now the screen has ingeniously attempted to make us forget the stage."[18]

While I generally agree with Bazin's views, I must remind the reader that, for instance, in his *Othello* (1952), Welles successfully used natural settings and all the other resources and even "tricks" of filmmaking. Sacha Guitry, the celebrated French playwright, actor, and cinema director of the '30s and '40s, added many cinematic effects to the film versions of his own plays. We could certainly draw up a list of silly adaptations of plays for the silver screen. Jean Cocteau quotes in his *Diaries* the case of a screenwriter who wrote a shooting-script of *Romeo and Juliet*. After reading it, the producer asked, "Are you sure this is Shakespeare's play?" The writer answered with a grin, "I had to introduce some changes. Shakespeare had overlooked and missed several charming things."[19]

I think that, notwithstanding his love and deep understanding of cinema, Bazin, like most French intellectuals, basically remained faithful to the written and printed word, especially in the form of theatrical plays. He probably would have been horrified by the pretense of some stage directors to be auteurs. I wonder how he would have reacted to the relatively recent controversy over their role. Indeed, directors such as Peter Brook and Robert Wilson are not simply playwright's adjutants. They are creative people in their own right!

When I first came to New York in the fall of 1965 as a delegate to the United Nations, I had the chance to discover the American theatrical *avant-garde*, which was thriving under the guidance of a number of young artists. I was becoming somehow estranged from the world of cinema. Most of my friends in the New Wave were already operating inside the system and *Cahiers du Cinéma* was no longer defending the positions we had developed up to the mid-1960s. In the fall of 1966, I was thrilled to spend many days with Roberto Rossellini in New York. He had been invited to present his *Rise of Louis XIV* at the New York Film Festival. As usual, he was less interested in cinema than in social changes. We explored together the world of the "hippies" and other "drifters." We saw a number of happenings. After his departure, the guide assigned to him by the Festival, Jeannie Richards, took me to some avant-garde shows. I also met Ninon Karlweis, the widow of the Austrian-born actor, then a theatrical agent, who had brought Jerzy Grotowski to the United States. She introduced me to Bob Wilson, who was showing his *Deafman's Glance*. I became a regular patron of the Café-La Mama and other off-off-Broadway stages. I saw *Paradise Now* (Living Theater, Julian Beck); *Doctor Selavy's Magic Theater* (Richard Foreman's ontological-hysteric theater); *Dance Theater* (Alwin Nikolais); *Dionysus in 69* (Richard Scheshner's Performance Group); *The Moondreamers* (Julie Bovasso); *Eye in New York* (Tom Eyen–John Vaccaro); *Alice* (André Gregory); *Wanton Soup* (Ching Yeh); *Bluebeard* (Charles Ludlam's Ridiculous Theatrical Company); and many more. In short, the '60s and '70s were a period of seething creativity in the performance arts in New York.

What struck me was that most of the productions revealed a shift from text to image. The "cinematic" influence was clear in all these experiments and more so in Grotowski's and especially Bob Wilson's pieces. Obviously, in that kind of theater, the role of the directors overshadowed that of playwrights and even actors! I wish Bazin could have witnessed all these trends. Maybe he would have shared some of the ideas developed by David Richard Jones, himself a stage director, in the late '80s: "I am inclined to accept the historical fact that directors have become central to modern theater and then to consider a corollary that modern theater is no doubt more sophisticated and more artistic for that change."[20] To him, a stage director is a genuine artist who creates original matter out of his own imagination. Jones repeats the famous remark by Vsevolod Meyerhold: "Words in theater are only a design on the canvas of motion." He adds that theater is nothing but a nexus of symbols—many of them visual—and dramatic literature cannot find its true form until embodied in the stage imagery of inspired directors. Robert Wilson, Joseph Chaikin, Peter Brook, Jerzy Grotowski, Richard Foreman, Andrei Serban, and their peers are real auteurs. Grotowski went as far as to write: "I believe that a dramatic script should provide only a theme for the director who will use it as the basis for a new, independent work or theater production."[21] Such contentions naturally enraged many actors and playwrights, who called stage directors "usurpers."

I developed a special friendship with Bob Wilson, who at the time used his SoHo loft to present his early productions in the making. I even worked with him, bringing new ideas. I encouraged him in creating *The Life and Times of Joseph Stalin* and *Einstein on the Beach*. It seemed to me that he was producing with his "new" theater what the New Wave filmmakers had failed to do in the realm of cinema. He was searching for "images" and "movement" instead of text. In the same period, I saw the scenic adaptation of *Alice in Wonderland* by André Gregory who had based his piece on movement (almost like one of the old "chase" movies!).

It seems to me that the role of a stage director, far from fading, has grown larger in today's theater. Reporting in 1997 from Paris, Alan Riding wrote, "These are not happy days for theater in Europe. Everywhere top actors fear losing lucrative TV and film work if they sign up for the full run of a play. Audiences are graying because young people find movies and rock concerts more fun than theater. Almost by default, responsibility for drawing audiences back to theater has now passed to directors. And here new faces and impressive new talents continue to rise" (*New York Times*, January 12, 1997).

Coming back to the film adaptation of plays, it seems to me that one should consider the filmmaker's intentions. If he considers the text as "sacred," he might, as Bazin said of Welles's *Macbeth* and Wyler's *The Little Foxes*, limit the cinematic "expansiveness" and highlight the actors' voices. On the other hand, he might also, as in the case of novels, just borrow the story, the plot. But even when he uses the text—the words of the playwright—the film director remains the auteur of his film. Thus, in 1977, having finished editing *Equus* and then starting on *The Wiz*, Sidney Lumet lamented the words of critics who accused him of "just filming stage plays." He told Tom Burke, who interviewed him,

Nonsense. Never have I done *plays on screen* unless I know what I can reveal about human behavior, emotional mechanisms, that I couldn't reveal without a camera! Peter Shaffer came to my Easthampton place [and] we talked endlessly. I still didn't know how a movie could *add* something. Then one day at a meeting, Tony Walton the scenic designer said, "In the boy's hospital room set, will you want a ceiling? Because if you have one, you could try that thing where he is lying in bed and a car passes outside, and the windshield reflects overhead." And I thought, "My God, that's what the movie is about." As a kid I'd never believed that that passing reflection was what I knew it was! I always let it be slightly frightening, mysterious. Suddenly, I knew that's how the movie could reinforce something that mattered hugely in the play thematically—the duality of everything! Nothing's quite what you expect it to be! That if *Equus* is about something, it's about duality, Jekyll and Hyde, Appolonian versus Dionysan thought, the double-edged sword we all carry! Creativity and its counterpart, our capacity for destruction.[22]

Suddenly he knew how to film the play! Asked if he had augmented the play, Lumet answered, "Nothing's missing on that stage, it is simply back to the definition of "movie." With the camera's reality, we could explore areas no stage could!"

In addition to the question of adaptation, we should also consider the relationship between theater and film from other angles. A 1999 one-man show by David Hare, *Via Dolorosa* gave Henry Grunwald, the former editor-in-chief of *Time*, an opportunity to comment on the "power of word" and the "balance between word and image" (*Wall Street Journal*, May 19, 1999). In *Via Dolorosa*, the author-performer David Hare talks for ninety minutes about a trip to Israel and his interviews with people and politicians. Grunwald writes, "This is no mere travelogue, nor merely a verbal version of a TV 'magazine' show with snippets strung together. It is a re-creation of life." He laments the tendency of TV journalism to drown us in pictures. In his opinion, we must keep in mind the "limitations of the camera." He concludes his remarks in the following manner. "As constant consumers of images, we should understand that, yes, pictures tell the truth—up to a point—but that only language can come close to telling the whole truth. One leaves David Hare's performance with the conviction that one word can be worth a thousand pictures." During my term as ambassador to the United Nations, I often met Henry Grunwald. He is a very cultured and intelligent writer and journalist. But like many authors of his generation he seems to lean toward the superiority of written and spoken language or at least to confuse the "uses" and "misuses" of the camera. The "superficiality" of TV news or TV news magazines has nothing to do with the images *per se*, but rather with the low level of spoken commentaries given or questions posed by the journalists, and, of course, with the arbitrary (if not intentional) choice and editing of the images. I am sure that if a TV commentator had ninety minutes to explain an event with words and images, she would be able to inform the viewers in depth! But news programmers allow only a few minutes, if not seconds, for each item! It is not ludicrous when a TV interviewer says to his guests: "We have twenty seconds left. What final thoughts can you give our viewers?" Moreover, theatrical shows like *Via Dolorosa* cannot be compared to TV news. They should rather be likened to film documentaries and travelogues.

Cocteau, in his diaries (March 23, 1942) wrote that cinema was the opposite of theater because film actors should not "play" their part but rather "think" it: They should speak softly and *let the camera do the rest* (by that he meant that close-ups and various film techniques would convey the meaning of the "play"). If we compare the role of the audiences of both arts, we have to admit that the theatergoer's role is somehow more active than that of the film viewer. Indeed, theatergoers have a kind of "silent dialogue" with the actors who are real people, not images on a screen. Theatergoers have ways to make actors feel as if they have convinced the audience or not. Their applause or lack of reaction at the end of an act or the end of the play is the direct expression of a judgment. Film producers and directors await the box-office figures, which never reflect the real feelings of the audience. Indeed, buying a ticket doesn't mean that you enjoyed a film!

Film has had a deep impact on theater by luring away a large part of its audiences. As the French drama critic and writer, Georges Charensol, put it in a 1931 article: "All the outward attractions [theater] has to offer will be found in the cinema in an intensified degree, accompanied by a profusion which the theatric super-productions of the boulevards could never rival."[23] The avant-garde companies, for their part, have tried to adopt some of the cinematic techniques, especially in the domains of lighting and creating the impression of movement. But, for all their innovative and brilliant efforts, neither a Wilson nor a Brook has succeeded in mustering as large a public as filmmakers! But the avant-garde has been able to create new forms of participation "theater" in which the audience can interact, whereas film as yet remains incapable of interaction with its viewers, despite the new computer technologies.

Charensol titled his 1931 article "The Death of the Theater" and wrote, "It may be that the day is close at hand when, having destroyed the theater, the cinema will supplant literature as well, and when the novelist will be no more than a cog in the vast motion-picture factory." More than half a century after these lines were published, literature and theater are still with us. They have undergone changes, their audiences have shrunk. Nevertheless they are alive and well!

Sidney Lumet, for one, doesn't believe in the end of theater and playwriting, although he believes that cinema enjoys superior advantages. Speaking about *Equus*, he said, "You can't bring real horses onto the stage. And while this problem was solved magnificently on Broadway—imaginary horses—I knew that in the movie, if the boy's wild horse ride was to have its full impact, the horror of the blinding must be graphic. It is and the ride's incredible! Orgasmic and real! Four-and-a-half minutes at full gallop, one uninterrupted shot, got it in one take!"

Toward the end of the interview, Tom Burke asked Lumet's opinion about the auteur theory. Here is Lumet's comment: "A picture a director's property? Patently ridiculous! *Network* is Paddy Chayefsky's life concept, I just preserved it. I am dependent on 170 people when I do a picture. The *weather* will change a scene's emotion, how much control do I ever have, finally? Personal pictures? That's about gossip! Listen, George Cukor's are personal movies. I know from them what he feels, and not one shot in any of 'em is autobiographical. Ingmar Bergman's highly personal, but geniuses have their own rules, we can learn nothing from Bergman but how inadequate the rest of us are." Yet in the same interview he also said: "To me, doing a picture, there's one question to which you *can't* leave yourself vulnerable—'How do we do that?' Or else 'they' are doing your picture, the technicians!" This repartee is somehow curious in the mouth of someone who doesn't consider himself an auteur! I must note that Lumet was never considered a real *auteur* by the critics of *Cahiers du Cinéma*. An excellent technician, yes. An auteur, no!

9

The Director as Author

In the never-ending debate over cinema and literature, writers always insist—with pride if not hubris—that they are the sole crafters of their books whereas the making of a film involves contributions from many people: actors, scenarists, electricians, cinematographers, art directors, sound engineers, editors, and so on. The director is but one of the specialists involved. True, but not the whole truth: Because of the multiplicity of collaborators, film badly needs a "unifier," a responsible person capable of giving it the essential element of cohesion without which it would be erratic and incomprehensible. This person is the director and her work is one of the most artistically "creative." Now, all directors are not "creators" (the same applies to the book world!). Some are mere technicians without any basic contribution. Consider, for instance, the Marx brothers movies, in which the actors enjoy a great deal of freedom and actually themselves create the entire show! Moreover, as it happens, some directors are mere *illustrators* of scripts. Only the great ones bring to the film their own view of the world, their own interpretation of a story, their own style.

By bestowing the authorship of a film on its director, we, in *Cahiers du Cinéma*, did not mean to ignore or downgrade the contributions of the scriptwriter or the cinematographer. The former, even when a renowned novelist, submits a "sketch," a "skeleton" to be fleshed out by the director. As Carl Dreyer used to say, the script should be considered as a draft, on which the director continues to work before and during the shooting. Moreover, if the scriptwriter would direct himself, his film, in all probability, would not resemble that of the director! In remakes, the new version of the same story never matches earlier ones. Each director puts his imprint on the script and the end-product is always different. As for the cinematographer, whose contribution is indeed very important (without it, there would be no film to project on the silver screen!), if she were to direct the movie herself, hers would also differ from the director's. A young American filmmaker of the 1970s epitomized the role of the director in the following words: "A filmmaker uses people and equipment as tools to make an expression of himself" (Jim McBride, quoted by Joseph Gelmis).

Critics of the director-author theory remark that, in films such as *Anna Karenina* or *The Dead* (made by John Huston after James Joyce's short story "The Dubliners"), one finds numerous "scenes" from the adapted book. Indeed, scenes are part of the story borrowed by the film, but not elements of the author's style. If Tolstoy or Joyce had produced movies instead of writing stories, would their visual treatment of the scenes in question be the same as that of Clarence Brown or John Huston?

The idea of film *authorship* goes back to the beginnings of cinema. Everyone, for instance, considered Chaplin and Griffith, to name just two, the *authors* of their own movies. Despite heavy studio interference in the work of moviemakers in the '30s, '40s, and part of the '50s, voices airing the thesis of director-author were heard from time to time. Thus, in its November 1946 issue, the French monthly magazine *La Revue du Cinéma* published an article by the Hollywood director Irving Pichel titled "Creation Must Be the Work of One Person." After a private screening of Jean Delannoy's *L'Assassin A Peur La Nuit*, Cocteau noted in his diary, "What is lacking as usual is the presence of an auteur of a soul" (May 20, 1942). About the same time, Orson Welles said, "I believe a work is good to the degree that it expresses the man who created it" (quoted by François Truffaut in his book *Films of My Life*). In 1948, the young French director Alexandre Astruc coined the term *camera-stylo*, meaning that the filmmaker should use his camera as the writer uses his pen.[24]

So, my comrades and I in the celebrated French magazine *Cahiers du Cinéma* did not invent the theory of authorship in the '50s. We merely adopted it and spread it among film fans. Our novelty consisted in developing its underlying concept of mise-en-scène (film direction) as the means by which the director conveys his style and viewpoint. In our reviews we considered "strong" directors (those capable of projecting their convictions in their work) as the ultimate authorities and sole arbiters of their movies' meaning and intention. On this template, Truffaut developed his *politique des auteurs*, which was something else. Indeed, it consisted in *defending and lauding without distinction all the films* of a director considered an auteur. As Bazin cautioned at the time, this amounted at introducing a "cult of personality" inside film criticism! One has to agree with Orson Welles's assessment: "We've all been brainwashed, for some two centuries, into servility in the presence of Genius as Cult Hero. The true importance of an artist is judged not by how much he impresses us, but by the gifts we receive from him. Shakespeare and Molière opened windows; they were liberators. The ego-licensed Cult Hero is an invader. He breaks in and—drunk with the sound of breathless praise—burns the house."[25] Truffaut's was, in fact, a *calculated* policy, promoted and practiced by a group of young critics introduced by him in *Cahiers du Cinéma*. It was by no means a theory of cinema, nor the general "line" of all *Cahiers* writers. It appeared for the first time in a February 1955 article in which Truffaut praised *Ali Baba*, one of the least defensible of Becker's movies. It subsided in the mid-1960s. Auteurism, by contrast, spread all over the world and survived in different forms.

In the early '60s, in the United States, Andrew Sarris followed suit and proclaimed his own *author* theory, which differed slightly from ours. Thirty years after the publication of Sarris's views in *Film Culture* in New York, I attended a panel discussion on the *author* theory, organized by the Film Society of Lincoln Center and the Directors Guild of America. Sarris seemed somewhat tamed and apologetic. He acknowledged having "underestimated the importance of screenwriters" and added that the theory worked best when it looked back, through film history, rather than trying to identify the "geniuses of tomorrow." As a *New York Times* reporter put it, "Like many a young radical, the auteur theory enters the middle age with a slight paunch, thinning hair and a decided air of respectability."[26] As for our group of critics in *Cahiers du Cinéma*, I must say that we were aware of our own "exaggerations." But how one can spread a relatively new opinion by sitting on the fence instead of plunging headlong in the battlefield?

In hindsight, I think the battle was won and that we might now give to each movie technician the credit she deserves. No longer does anyone question the major role and responsibility of the director (a "good" one, it goes without saying!). No one except some angry screenwriters! For instance, in a book titled *Monster: Living off the Big Screen* (New York, 1996), the novelist John Gregory Dunne recounted the difficulties he encountered as a scripwriter in Hollywood. After interviewing him and some others, Bernard Weinraub wrote, "Screenwriters seem to spend shocking amounts of time complaining about their not-so-tragic plight . . . and the complaints can ring hollow . . . William Faulkner, Nathaniel West, F. Scott Fitzgerald, Dorothy Parker and Clifford Odets signed on in the 1930's and 1940's. They drank a lot, did not write too many movies, made some money and whined that Hollywood was awful" (*The New York Times*, February 2, 1997).

In recent years, the ego of scriptwriters, among other contributors to the film industry, has been on the rise. Indeed, with the impact of new technologies (cable, satellite, computer, the Internet, and so on), the number of television channels and other viewing posts is steadily multiplying. As a result, demand for stories, teleplays and screenscripts is swelling. Screenwriting courses are sprouting up in universities as well in continuing-education schools. Robert McKee, author of *Story: Substance, Structure, Style and the Principles of Screenwriting* (New York, 1997), told interviewer Don Oldenburg that the "screenwriting impulse" is heightened because "movies have emerged from the shadow of the novel and stage play as the premier storytelling medium. . . . We finally realized film is the defining art form of the 20th century. People's love of it, their understanding of it, grows with every decade, and their appreciation of the art of screenwriting grows, too" (*The Washington Post*, February 10, 2000). Therefore, one should understand the "anger" of screen-writers.

I remember that in 1989, Budd Schulberg, who certainly is one of the greatest "scenarists" in the United States (and probably in the world), vehemently protested and asked, "Why do film di-rectors get more credit than writers?" This was, if I am not mis-taken, at the occasion of the literary award bestowed on him by the jury of the American Cinema Festival in Deauville, France.[27] Here is an excerpt from his acceptance speech: "My impression of the auteur theory is that of a giant vacuum cleaner sucking up all the contributions of the writers (not to mention the cam-eramen and film editors) into one great overblown bag labeled auteur-director." Schulberg added, "Did Ford write *Stagecoach, The Informer* or *The Long Voyage Home*? No, it was the gifted Dud-ley Nichols who, in each case, built his adaptations on writers as preeminent in their own field as Ernest Hycox, Sean O'Faolain, and Eugene O'Neill." ("The 'Auteur Syndrome,' " *The New York Times*, December 4, 1989). Indeed, an excellent script can become either a good or a bad movie, depending on the talent of the director! The script is not the film, even when the director follows it step by step. Robbe-Grillet's script for Alain Resnais's *L'Année Dernière á Marienbad* is a case in point. Resnais did not change it. He had participated in its collaboration at every stage but had left the writing to the novelist who pub-lished it under his own name. Yet, reading it does not convey an idea of the images that appear on the screen! Once more we must recognize and keep in mind the basic fact that *words cannot be images*. As I already remarked by quoting Dreyer, in the best case, a scenario is a kind of *blueprint* that the director often changes according to his needs. Roberto Rossellini once told me that he fleshed out the lines of the screenplay in his head and never used a typed script. I asked him, "Then, why do you bother to hire a scriptwriter and print many copies of the written script?" He answered, "It is for the producers. Producers who put up or find the money are reassured by the existence of a detailed script. They hardly read it." Over the years I learned not to take Rossellini's statements at face value. He always worked with scriptwriters. Indeed, I myself contributed part of the script of *India* in 1958. But he would change many things during the shooting. Screenwriters often suggest important ideas to the director who incorporates them in his own conception of the story. In retrospect, I would compare the movie screenwriter to a politician's speechwriter. No matter how many of the speechwriter's ideas are retained, the final speech is the politician's views, not her writer's! JFK's famous line "Ask not what your country can do for you . . ." remains in history as a JFK's phrase, not his speechwriter's!

Our auteur theory of the '60s became especially fashionable after some writers of *Cahiers du Cinéma*, such as Truffaut, Chabrol, Rohmer, and Godard produced their first feature films. All of a sudden, numerous young directors' names invaded the credits on the silver screen. As a result, besides the movie star, another "sacred monster" shone in the skies the director-author. In fact, we had prepared the terrain. For years, we had patiently demonstrated that some of the directors of Hollywood's B-movies were real auteurs. Many people laughed at us. "How could this be possible in the 'studio system' where the producer and the studio tycoons controlled the final cut of movies?" We scrupulously analyzed the movies and showed that many filmmakers had been able to put their "personal" stamp and style into films made under the "impersonal" Hollywood factory conditions of the '30s and '40s! We drew attention to the craft and creativity of Ernst Lubitsch, Josef von Sternberg, Fritz Lang, Nicholas Ray, Vincent Minelli, Douglas Sirk, Frank Tashlin, and many others. I, for one, am proud to have been part of the movement during the '50s and '60s that helped to stimulate new interest in cinema as an art and in directors as authors. By the early '60s the auteur concept was well established, if not yet a household word! Roman Polanski, whose ego knows no bounds, unabashadly proclaimed, "The director is always a *superstar*. The best films are best because of nobody but the director. You speak of *Citizen Kane* or *Eight and a Half* or *Seven Samurai*, it's thanks to the director who was the star of it. He makes the film. He creates it" (quoted by Joseph Gelmis in his book *The Film Director as Super-Star*, 1970).

The supremacy of directors in the '60s and '70s has waned somewhat in recent years; actors are climbing to the top of the industry's ladder once again. But old habits die hard. Even in Hollywood's most commercial films, the credits start with the phrase "A film by . . .". Yet, by the standards of the '50s and '60s, motion pictures like *Jurassic Park* or *48 Hours*, to single out just two box-office hits, could not be considered auteur movies. Even if the auteur theory has lost its meaning in today's cinema, the pre-eminence of directors seems to survive as we witness the explosion of books about them. True, these books are less about their art than about their private lives. Nevertheless, they illustrate the idea of the director as star, which, according to Caryn James, was born of "a marriage between auteurism and the media-mad culture of celebrity."[28] The trend is in such vogue that some "cultists" have dug up the tomb of the World's Worst Director and resuscitated his body (!) of "work." In 1992, Tim Burton made a movie about the horror pictures director *Ed Wood*, after a biography written by Rudolph Grey.[29] As critic Richard Corliss noted, "Wood was, no question, a stupefyingly inept director."[30] But he left the imprint of his particular kind of ineptitude (if one may say so) in his pictures! Can the opposite of an author be an author by *reductio ad absurdum*? My late friend Ado

Kyrou once wrote, "Learn to go see the *worst* films. They are sometimes sublime."[31] He was a member of the surrealist group!

Be that as it may, the concept of the director as auteur has somehow survived in film culture. The most respectable *New York Times* dedicated a whole editorial to Stanley Kubrick on his death ("The Edgy Legacy of Stanley Kubrick," March 10, 1999). It stated that Hollywood found Kubrick "an unquantifiable sum, a man driven by perfectionism and the ideal of artistic control in an art form where collaboration, not to say compromise, is the rule. . . . What Kubrick's choice of projects reveals is a keen literacy . . . and a taste for the extremes of logic, the conclusions our culture's unexamined premises lead us to . . . The visions that get at difficult truths are not usually the ones that soothe us, and those were Kubrick's." In 1984 the same newspaper published Truffaut's obituary on its front page! This would not have happened before the developments of the '60s and '70s! Today filmmakers have become as important as politicians and other celebrities!

The auteurism fashion highly irritated Orson Welles, though he himself had been our poster boy for the auteur theory. In a scathing article, published in 1970, he derided it and ridiculed some of the most famous directors of his time. He thus dubbed Antonioni a "solemn architect of empty boxes" and wrote about Fellini: "In place of the old movie star, there towers over us now another sacred monster: the Great Director (an allusion to Chaplin's *The Great Dictator*?). As far as popular mythology is concerned, when Fellini hired his country's foremost male star to play Fellini in a Fellini film about Fellini—his *Eight and a Half*— the sun may be said to have set on the day of the actor. In this epoch the glamour is mostly behind the camera."[32]

Orson Welles was a director as well as an actor. As a director, he had been out of business for some time so he might have been somewhat biased. Therefore, his opinions can be challenged. John Barrymore used to say that great directors would always discuss their views with their actors whom they expected to contribute "intelligently" to the making of the movie. By contrast, Antonioni thought that film actors should not "under-stand" their part, but merely follow the director's instructions. He dismissed as illusory any real "collaboration" between actors and directors, in his view, the actor is a kind of Trojan Horse in the director's domain (*L'Express*, Paris, February 2, 1961). It is also said that Hitchcock despised his actresses. But this has nothing to do with auteurship.

10

Filmmakers Haunted by Literature

The very word *auteur* is borrowed from the other arts, especially literature. Filmmakers have always been attracted by literature. As their profession was considered somewhat trivial and they themselves viewed as sheer entertainers, they looked at novelists with envy. In order to gain "respectability," they tapped into the literary treasures of the past and the present; they adapted and used the titles of masterpieces.

Even now, when cinema has established itself as an art form in its own right, a number of filmmakers are still haunted by literature. Not content that image-in-motion has become a language of its own (in the sense of spoken and written languages), they seem determined to dispossess the literary language of what belongs to it. I am thinking, for instance, of the work of an Antonioni or a Godard. In this quest, filmmakers follow the opposite road taken by many contemporary novelists and arrive at the same impossibility: Images cannot become words (and vice versa). That is, signs having *fixed* meanings In *L'Avventura*, as in *La Notte*, for example, Antonioni's purpose is to signify through images his characters' "interior," their state of mind. He sets himself an unattainable goal: the synthesis of subjective and objective, of "interior" and "exterior." But instead of succeeding in showing the "interior" of his heroes, he produces a plethora of what in music are called "rests." The protagonists (respectively, Monica Vitti and Jeanne Moreau) wander aimlessly around an island or on the streets of a city and gaze at the surroundings in long sequences in which nothing happens.

Alternating between description and introspection, the novelist can *at will* throw light on her characters from *outside* and from *inside*. She can, as it were, both *photograph* and *radiograph* her protagonists. Film, by contrast, can only show the exterior! In order to communicate to the spectator what is going inside the minds of actors, cinema has to resort to theatrical means—dialogue and soliloquy. Or it has to use artificial tricks such as commentary or voice over, as Godard and others usually do. Godard goes as far as to add quotations from his preferred books to the sound track. Some of his films were loaded with so much commentary and so many voiceovers that I dubbed them "movies for the blind"!

Almost everybody agrees that Luchino Visconti's *Death in Venice* (1971) (after Thomas Mann's novella on the few last months in the life of a writer at the peak of his craft) is a masterpiece. The slow-moving story is mainly located in the "mind" of the hero, played by Dirk Bogarde. The Italian master changed him into a music composer because, in his opinion, musicians are easier to cast in a film than writers: You can add the music to the sound track, while for a novelist you have to resort to noncinematic devices such as the voiceover or commentaries. Visconti succeeded in making the audience share the interior passion that consumes the main character of a film almost totally lacking in action and movement!

Adapting a James Joyce short story for *The Dead* (1987), John Huston confronted the story's numerous forays into the mind of the principal character, Gabriel. Although he tried to use images, he could not avoid off-camera commentaries. Let me take as an example the dinner-table sequence. Joyce had this to say: "[Gabriel] felt quite at ease now, for he was an expert carver and liked nothing better than to find himself at the head of a well-laden table." Joyce also minutely described the food on the table. The camera lingers over the plates, the spoons, the forks, the knives, the glasses, and so on. The shot of the goose's carcass underscores the high quality of the dinner: The guests did not leave over even a shred of meat! But despite the astute "image equivalences" of Joyce's remarks and descriptions, Huston could not avoid off-camera commentaries. All in all, his efforts at "cinematization" (if I may use such a word) stretched the movie to two hours while the short story was under fifty pages!

Actually, off-camera commentaries have frequently been used by filmmakers and their scriptwriters, especially in adaptations of private-eye stories such as those of Raymond Chandler and Mickey Spillane. I, for one, find them somehow redundant because the images often seem self-explanatory. They also raise another question: Voiceovers use the past tense, while what we see on the screen tends to appear at the present tense! To create and underscore the impression of the past, filmmakers usually resort to costumes, settings, and a combination of various other devices.

Be this as it may, I remember that in the early '60s, when my comrades at *Cahiers du Cinéma* abandoned film criticism to go behind the camera and launch what came to be known as the New Wave, they were accused of introducing a certain "literary style" into cinema. Several aspects of their work were viewed as inherent to the book world: autobiography in Truffaut's films; book quotations in Godard's, "precious" dialogues in Rohmer's; dialogues and scripts by well-known novelists in Resnais's. This really amounted to ascribing a special meaning to the word "literary" in the case of my friends' films; in fact, far from confining themselves to a "verbalism" that defined the works of many of their predecessors, they actually pioneered innovations in the use of the camera, as well as in editing, dialogue, and acting. In more ways than one, they helped liberate the world of cinema from what we used to call the "imperialism" of literature!

The New Wave label was deceptive. While one can regard it as corresponding to a more or less coherent movement that began around 1960, one must still make it clear that this movement was short lived. Very quickly its champions became directors whose films differed greatly from one another as well as from those of their predecessors. In addition, most of them joined the mainstream cinema they used to denounce and deride when they wrote reviews! Nonetheless, the movement that sprang up in France left an imprint on world cinema and influenced other young directors in many countries, including the United States. A couple of decades ago, referring to the then–new generation of American filmmakers, Mervyn LeRoy, a Hollywood non-author director, said that one could no longer go to the movies without taking along a box of aspirin! (At the time Tylenol had not yet gained its present fame!) Responding to him, I wrote in one of my shortest articles, "Feel free, Mr. LeRoy! Help the aspirin industry!"

I must add that when I was writing about cinema in the Paris of the '50s and '60s, I had no idea that our bickerings and polemics would influence film appreciation and film production to such a profound degree. My involvement in *Cahiers du Cinéma* and other magazines such as *Positif* and *Fiction*, was a kind of hobby. I was therefore amazed when I was recently invited to lecture at Iowa State University on my involvement with the defunct New Wave and on the new Iranian cinema. To my surprise, I found that students were analyzing our articles of the '50s and '60s. I was shown books published by Harvard University and other educational centers on *Cahiers du Cinéma*. I must confess to some mixed feelings on that account. On the one hand, I had become part of the history of cinema, an old chap, a survivor! On the other hand, what was written and published about our doings in *Cahiers du Cinéma* did not reflect the fun that animated us at the time. But that is another story.

11

Cinema and Technology

At this point, I would like to pause for a short moment and come back to what I said at the start about dreams (including daydreams) and cinema. The kinship between them had struck me since childhood and later influenced my views about film appreciation. I gradually came to consider cinema as the *exteriorization* of our natural faculty of using moving images as a means of expression in our nightly visions. The Lumières' and Edison's inventions made this *exteriorization* possible in the last decade of the nineteenth century. I was not astonished when Luis Buñuel told us, during a visit to Paris, that the images of his films originated in his dreams *Un Chien Andalou* (1928) was actually based on two dreams! Salvador Dali dreamt of a handful of running ants and Buñuel of a razor cutting the moon in two pieces: His scriptwriter of the 1970s, the French novelist Jean-Claude Carrière, confirmed that Buñuel always introduced dream sequences in his films. Take, for instance, the group walking in the street and meeting a dead person in *The Discreet Charm of the Bourgoisie* (1972), or, from Buñuel's earlier period Robinson dreaming of his father in *The Adventures of Robinson Crusoe* (1952).

Over the years new inventions allowed the introduction of sound, color, wide screen (cinemascope), multiple-focal lenses, and the like. Obviously, all this had an impact on filmmaking and provoked changes in every aspect of cinema. Even directors participated in the flurry of inventions. Thus, Roberto Rossellini conceived a monitoring device that allowed him to command the multiple-focal lense of the camera from his directorial seat without looking into the viewer and giving instructions to his cameraman! As our common friend, Enrico Fulchignoni, re-marked at the time, "This stems directly from his laziness. Now he is able to direct movies without leaving his chair!" (Indeed, Rossellini disliked physical effort! He even developed a theory linking Italians' so-called "indolence" to the Romans whose stat-ues represented heroes seated on or leaning against something, while in Greece and other nations heroes stood erect!)

In any case after World War II the spread of new technologies such as television and satellite communications influenced cin-ema both in the production and the screening of films. Theater audiences shrank as middle-aged and older people tended to remain at home in front of their small screens. Hollywood shifted much toward catering to teenagers' tastes. "Multiplexes" sprouted up all over the world.

Later on, with cable and satellite TV, hundreds of supplemen-tary channels invaded living rooms. Film producers continued to look at the development of television only in terms of box-office earnings. Yet the tremendous increase in the number of TV viewers influenced the very style of filmmaking. Indeed, on the silver screen the enlarged image brought the smallest detail to the attention of the spectator. It was as if you were looking at the actors and settings through magnifying glasses. Each facial expression, each object, each gesture, each detail, conveyed a "message" to the audience. The story (its "meaning" or "mes-sage") was, so to speak, buried in the images. Dialogue could be considered as superfluous or was used to complete or underline the message. Obviously, on the small screen most of this is lost and therefore frequent close-ups and expanded dialogue become indispensable for the understanding of a story. In some respects, one can say that TV's style is closer to that of theater than to that of cinema. Speech dominates TV films as well as sitcoms, news programs, documentaries, and so on. Hence the success of talk shows!

The growing importance of TV in the entertainment industry, in turn, impacts the cinema industry, as studios produce more and more films destined for the small screen. At the same time, screenwriters, with their better-organized Guild, are gaining power both in TV and in cinema. As a result of all these trends, movies are becoming more talky than ever, if not totally verbose! One effect is redundancy: The images and the lines spoken by actors (or included in off-camera commentaries) often duplicate one another! Many a new movie become more bearable on the small screen while older movies remain more rewarding on the silver one! Even perfectly produced and directed yarns, like some Hitchcock's or Ford's, lose steam on the TV screen! But then, with the rapid development of larger TV projection systems, larger screens (sixty inches and over) are entering the living rooms (of people who can afford them!). In time, this will certainly affect the format, content, and style of TV programs, whose gaps are often filled in with cinema.

I do not intend to embark here on a study of the reciprocal impacts of TV on cinema and vice versa. I merely seek to point out that the wide dissemination of image through cable and satellite TV does not necessarily mean the death of speech, let alone of books. In order to answer some of the questions posed at the beginning of this book, we need to take into account the new technological trends. Already they have subtly altered both our way of life and our perception of the world. The well-known literary critic Sven Birkerts contends that their impact on our sense of knowledge might be "as transformative as the shift from Newtonian to Einsteinian physics" (*Readings*, New York, 1998). In any case, the rapid development of computer science has already had a profound impact on moviemaking. Digitally produced monsters and prehistoric animals as well as other cinematic "tricks," have transformed silly stories into box-office hits. Studios are relying more and more on computerized special effects! Indeed, it appears that "digital" effects go beyond classic "special effects," which did not affect the director's style. By contrast, computer wizards introduce their own style in the "effect" sequences! Their contribution to the overall movie is much more than that of choreographers in old "musicals"! On the other hand, computer "culture" is spreading rapidly and touching almost everybody. Film directors of the future will probably themselves be adept at using the new technology and regain their authority on "digitalized" films.

To be sure, it is difficult to prophesy in such an environment. In the early '60s, McLuhan announced the imminent death of books and what he dubbed the "Gutenberg Galaxy." Thirty years later the printed word and books are still alive and well! Yet despite the enduring presence on bestseller lists of Danielle Steele, Judith Kranz, John Grisham, and their ilk, people do read less. McLuhan's mistake was in trying to foresee the immediate future. He should have followed the example of the poet Apollinaire, who, musing over cinema in 1917, affirmed that books will die *in one or two centuries*! A century has almost passed Apollinaire still has a hundred years to go before anyone can belie his forecast! My point here is not to dismiss books and literature in comparison with the ever-rising power of new image-producing and -distributing tools. I just want to highlight the necessity of taking into account the development of new technologies in assessing the present and future relations among literature, film, and television shows. At the very least, after a century of cinema and almost fifty years of TV, we can say without fear of contradiction that the potential of images as a means of communication has not yet been fully realized. In order to further explore the evolution of film styles, it may prove useful to turn the reader's attention to the way audiences receive and react to the moving images displayed on the silver screen.

12

Different Ways of Looking at and Making Films

In my childhood I considered film theaters as places akin to temples. They were very special places where people usually kept silent in the dark and looked straight ahead at the screen, as if they were worshiping some Supreme Being. I remember my excitement every Saturday afternoon waiting for an adult to take me to the cinema. The line of people at the box office, the dim lights inside that gradually diminished, the slow opening of the curtain, the music, and the long-awaited images! A solemn ceremony that repeated itself each week like a special church or mosque liturgy. I revered all movies independent of their actors and content. They literally fascinated me. Back home the images lingered in my head and, once in bed, I "projected" whole sequences of what I had seen, on my "internal screen" until sleep would overwhelm me. Later on, during my adolescence and university years, I became more selective, but remained fanatic about the films I liked. I also cherished the pre-projection moments, when one prepares oneself to view the movie. It was then that it occurred to me that one could look at movies in different ways. I tried to sort them out and soon abandoned the chore as the list was growing longer and longer.

To sum up my "findings" from those days, I would say that

there are at least two ways of watching a film. First, by immersing themselves in it, spectators abandon themselves to the free play of what psychologists call "identification" and "projection." Spectators then become one with the characters or ascribe to them the spectators' own tendencies and experiences. They mentally put themselves, as it were, into the actor's skin, sharing the actor's feelings and actions. The other way of seeing a film consists in "opposing it," combating the "fascination" of the image, standing aloof from what is being presented on the screen. In this manner of looking at a film, one allows one's critical faculties to function even as the movie is unfolding. In this case spectators "watch" the actor without allowing themselves to get involved without taking sides in the conflicts that take place before their eyes. Viewers become judges presiding over a case in a courtroom! Then they experience a kind of pleasure in the "second degree," derived from *knowledge* and not from *identification* or emotion. (Actually, film critics should always adopt this manner of looking at a picture.)

It might be said that such a distinction also applies to reading a book. This is correct save for two exceptions. On the one hand, reading a book takes more than two hours. On the other, you can stop and then resume reading at any moment, while you are trapped for two hours in a movie theater! In any case, readers identify more easily with characters in novels than viewers identity with screen actors, because words cannot present the heroes as accurately and precisely as film images! Literary critics can keep their distance while reading a book more easily than movie critics can distance themselves from a film. Be this as it may, you can like a film (or part of it) in either of these ways, depending on whether you respond to the movie on an emotional level or you view it from a more intellectual perspective. It goes without saying that these two ways of receiving the film's "message" represent *extremes* or ideal poles between which, in reality, an infinity of possible combinations exists.

Similar poles can be found in filmmaking. Some directors appeal to viewers' emotions and others to their intellect. Some offer to spectators a mirror in which they can recognize themselves and easily identify with the main characters. In such films, the problems that beset the fictional protagonists are suggested vaguely rather than precisely defined, while their surroundings are shown in great detail. In this manner, the director, consciously or not, facilitates the phenomenon of *projection* on the part of the viewer. This technique is apparent in Michelangelo Antonioni's movies, including *L'Avventura, La Notte, Deserto Rosso, The Passenger,* and the like. The camera's commitment to objectivity makes it possible to downplay individual differences. In *La Notte,* for instance, the writer and his wife retain enough *generality* in their ill-defined problems of the moment (an unclear and early process of estrangement) to allow spectators to identify with them. I remember very well *L'Avventura's* critical and box-office triumph in Paris in 1960. I personally interviewed members of the audience as they left the theater. They all spoke of the "truth" of the characters and their problems, unaware that they had projected their own problems onto them! Indeed, the Italian filmmaker had not described the "problems" of his characters. Film critics spoke of the birth of "introspection cinema," characterized by a smooth and free narrative style and a mastery of technical devices! The relative "emptiness" of Antonioni's heroes eluded the spectators as well as the reviewers!

Another characteristic of directors like this is that they always insert *oases of tranquility* in their films—sequences in which nothing happens. This gives spectators ample time to project their own concerns onto the protagonists. Take, for instance, Jeanne Moreau's long walk in Antonioni's *La Notte.* A more recent example is Abbas Kiarostami's *The Taste of Cherry* (1998), which won the *Palme d'Or* at the Cannes Film Festival. The whole film consists of one car ride by the principal protagonist who is searching for a man to help him commit suicide! Well-to-do and upper middle class audiences hail such directors as "geniuses" because they think they recognize themselves—or at least part of their problems or some general "human" concerns—in these movies. "That's truth," they exclaim when the final credits roll on the silver screen. I deliberately say the well-to-do and the upper middle class, because the rest of the public is only bored, and for good reason. The settings (rich hosts in vast luxurious mansions, an expensive car in northern Tehran) are very different from their own.

Vincent Canby's review of *The Passenger* (1975) illustrates my point. I shall quote this passage:

> *The Passenger* is open to all sorts of solemn interpretations, a lot of them involving the use of the word "alienation" which may be the most boring word to gain wide currency in the last twenty years. Once you leave the film's narrative level to ponder its other meanings, you are on your own. *The Passenger* shouldn't be scrutinized and deciphered like a top secret NATO message. It is a poetic vision. Its images, as perfectly illuminated as a night landscape by a flash of lightning, suggest all sorts of associations, from "The Odyssey" to other movies, including hot-boiling, multi-national coproductions about Interpol agents. ("Antonioni's Haunting Vision," *New York Times*, April 20, 1975)

By contrast, other directors refuse to resort to these means and rack their brains to particularize situations and characters to such an extent that it becomes impossible for spectators to recognize themselves in them. At the same time, they eliminate dead spots, overload the settings, and require the viewers' attention at every moment. Specialists in suspense may be included in this category. Because they have to keep the audience on the edge of their seats, these directors try to introduce in their films a breathtaking rhythm, which leaves spectators no time for projection or identification. In that respect, Alfred Hitchcock may be considered a real master. In most of his movies he succeeds in grabbing viewers' attention and trapping them in the flow of suspense. Nothing he shows on the screen is unneccessary. To take one example, *Rear Window* remains perfect after almost half a century. In recent movies, one can cite Wolfgang Petersen, the director of *Das Boot* (1981) a nail-biting adventure about a German

U-Boat on a mission during World War II, *In the Line of Fire* (1993), and *Air Force One* (1997), with Harrison Ford playing the U.S. president taken hostage by a group of Russian terrorists. Petersen's extremely efficient direction goes beyond the apparent suspense and invites viewers to think after the movie ends. He even manages to insert the obligatory love scene without taking away from the suspense (as in *In The Line of Fire*)!

But directors don't need to tell suspense stories to join the group of filmmakers who reject resorting to projection and identification. Consider, as examples, Joseph Losey's films (*Eva, The Servant, Accident*, and the like). Losey himself told us in Paris in the late '50s: "As soon as emotion triumphs over reflection in the spectator, the director has failed." In this observation, one can detect the influence of Brecht's theory of *distanciation*. Indeed, Losey had been Brecht's assistant when Brecht came to the United States. In any event, one is compelled to concede that the characters in *Eva* (1964) or *The Secret Ceremony* (1968), not to mention *The Servant* (1963), are so peculiar that it becomes almost totally impossible to identify with them.

Obviously, neither Antonioni nor Losey belong exclusively to one group or the other. Here, too, there exists a whole range of possibilities and combinations between the extremes. In that perspective Francis Ford Coppola and Martin Scorcese are good examples of successful filmmakers who mix both ways of directing.

As I noted earlier, some may protest that the preceding remarks apply equally well to literature: The reader of a novel often identifies with the heroes. But there are writers who do not use the projection trap; instead, they prefer to force their readers to look at the characters from a distance. This similarity between the realms of cinema and literature should not astonish us. Indeed, both arts "tell" stories! A few novelists even propound the idea that a film is nothing more than a script in images.

13

Film Language?

Pier Paolo Pasolini, who was a poet, writer, and screenwriter before becoming, in the late '60s, one of the great post-war Italian directors, has given some thought to the question of the relation between movies and scenario. In the early '70s he summarized his views in several articles, one of which was published in *Cahiers du Cinéma*.[33] He asserted that film is based on a system of signs that is different from the written-spoken system. There is no correlate in film to the concept of "idiom" for the writer. There is no prior codified vocabulary for the cinematic esthetic enterprise. But since cinema is not a "monstrosity," since we "understand" movies, one must suppose the existence of *something* that does the job of words in literature. Pasolini proposed what he called "sign-images" as a collection of codifiable (but not yet codified) references that would enable spectators to understand communication by film. Filmmakers are compelled (unconsciously at least) to invent a "language," then an "art," whereas writers, having at their disposal the "written-spoken" system, are inventors only at the aesthetic level. According to Pasolini, then, there exists a "cinematic language" comparable to the literary one, but different from it.

Also in the '60s, the French linguist Christian Metz observed that cinema has never had a syntax or a grammar in the precise sense of linguistics, but that it obeys *fundamental semiological laws* (inherent in the deepest necessities of communication of any kind of information) which are difficult to formulate. A model of them should be sought in the area of *general semiology*. In other words, what is called the "grammar" of cinema is not a grammar in the proper sense of the term, but rather a collection of semantic implications, codified only in part. This is almost what the late French novelist Roger Martin Du Gard expressed much more simply in a letter to a friend a few years before he died. He characterized cinema as an "art without real contours, without well-tested rules, as it is without limit in its possibilities."

But a question arises here: How does it happen that spectators understand the cinematic "message" without any preparation, without any knowledge of the semiological "laws," whereas readers cannot read without first having studied the language and its grammar? This question had struck me since my childhood after my first filmic experiences. It occasionally popped back into my musings, especially after I started to write about film. It was then that I remembered how I had "solved" the "problem" in my early years in school by establishing a kinship between cinema and dreams. As I indicated earlier, in my opinion, cinema, in the form of nightly dreams and daydreaming, is a natural component of our brains. Therefore, we do not have to learn any special language or grammar to understand films.

Still, I personally don't mind concocting a theory of "film language." But if I were to express an opinion about the current theories, I must state that I prefer the revolutionary findings of Noam Chomsky over Metz's and Pasolini's ideas. To Chomsky, our comprehension and our perception of the world are based on *innate* ideas (such as *form, shape, movement*), and the principles of language exist in our minds since birth (the more than four hundred known languages are all founded on the same basic, genetically transmitted principles). He calls these principles *linguistic universals* or, in simpler terms, properties common to all languages. In his opinion, children know the principles of language before they are able to speak.

I think these ideas lend support to my early "intuition" about the relationship between dreams and films. Indeed, if spectators do not first have to learn the basic "rules" of cinematic expression, it is quite simply because they carry those rules within themselves as a result of their *natural* "oniric" activity and what Chomsky calls innate universals. If there is a "grammar," it is an "open grammar" that evolves and improves through the successive contributions of creative and original filmmakers. It would be pointless, even disastrous, to seek to codify the rules of filmmaking after the fashion of the rules of existing languages.

Here appears one of the essential differences between film and literature. Authors of novels rely on very precise rules codified once and for all. Filmmakers on the other hand, enjoy a great freedom in the organization of their images. In a way, they almost totally invent their own language with each film!

The conclusion that seems to emerge could be summarized in this way. Considered at their very foundations, cinematic "language" and literary language are based on one innate "fundamental grammar" dictated by the way in which human brain functions. But, when they progress toward "communicable" expression, the two "languages" separate because their "rules" cannot fuse!

Many specialists have tried, for instance, to compare "frames" to words and "sequences" to phrase. But the frame is not a word and the animated image is not a sentence! Curiously enough, Tolstoy well understood this basic difference between "moving images" and words. In the first pages of *Anna Karenina*, Prince Oblonsky suddenly jumps up from a pleasant slumber and opens his eyes, trying to remember his dream.

> What was it? Of course! Alabin was giving a dinner in Darmstadt, no, not in Darmstadt—somewhere in America. But that's where Darmstadt was, in America. So Alabin was

giving a dinner, on glass tables—and the tables were singing "Il mio tesoro," though not "Il mio tesoro" but something better, and there were some little decanters around
and they were really women, he remembered. Oblonsky's
eyes sparkled merrily; he smiled to himself as he sat thinking: Yes, it was great fun, all right. There were a lot of other
good things too, *but you can't put them into words*.

An extraordinary intuition of the basic difference between film
and literature, long before the invention of cinema! A precog-
nition, also, of the affinity between cinema and dream!

It is often said that film is based on a written script that details
each scene. But the scenario on which the director works differs
from the novel because, as Pasolini once wrote, it is a "form that
moves toward another form." Let me here go back to the article
by Anthony Burgess I quoted earlier. The author of *A Clockwork
Orange* affirmed: "I would rather write novels because in a novel
one is totally on one's own, and the intermediaries between oneself and the public are prepared to respect one's very word. My
publishers have corrected my spelling occasionally, and the prin-
ters have—probably not deliberately—perverted it, but they
have none of them tried to change the structure, the rhythm, the
dialogue, the characters. In this film world that temporarily ab-
sorbs me, there is too much collaboration, meaning too much
friction, and far too many people who would like to be writers
but are not." Burgess forgets one thing. The scenario he is writing is not the film! It will become film only by passing into another form through the whole process of direction, of what we
used to call mise-en-scène in our reviews and articles of the '50s
and '60s.

In a 1939 lecture and a 1963 interview, Alfred Hitchcock
clearly explained the amount and limits of the scriptwriter's contributions.[34] In his "English period," he used to work for weeks
with a writer until he reached a "complete narrative." Then he
would give the whole thing to a top writer to dialogue it. When

he came to the United States, he found that scenarists wouldn't go for that system of work. He did it verbally with the writer and afterwards made corrections and adjustments. Hitchcock told Peter Bogdanovich: "I would say I apply myself two-thirds before he [the screen writer] writes and one-third after he writes. But I will not and do not photograph anything he puts in the script on his own. . . . I mean any cinematic method of telling it—*how can he know*? On *North by Northwest*, Ernie Lehman wouldn't let me out of the office for a whole year. I was with him on every shot, every scene. Because it wasn't his material."[35]

Charlie Chaplin in *Modern Times* (1936).

From left: Aba Eban (Israel); Al Jamali (Iraq), who was executed three years later; and the author (Iran) voting on the text of the Universal Declaration of Human Rights in the Third Committee of the General Assembly of the U.N. (Paris, December 1948).

Raoul Walsh directing James Cagney in *A Lion in the Streets* (1953).

The author with director Ado Kyrou (left) in a surrealistic spoof in 1956 in Brussels.

Jean Renoir directing Ingrid Bergman and Jean Marais in *Paris Does Strange Things* (*Elena and Her Men*) (1956).

Jean Cocteau in Venice, Italy, 1956.

Robert Bresson is probably the paradigm of cinema "auteur."

Otto Preminger directing Richard Widmark in *Saint Joan* (1957).

Director Joseph Losey on the set of *Eva* (1960).

The author directing a documentary in Tehran, Iran in 1960. Pictured with cameraman Gounet.

From left to right: Alan Delyn (producer); Jacqueline Bisset; the author; François Truffaut; Shirley Clarke (American documentarist who died in 1997) at author's house in New York in 1972 when Truffaut was preparing to shoot *Night by Day* (*La Nuit Americaine*).

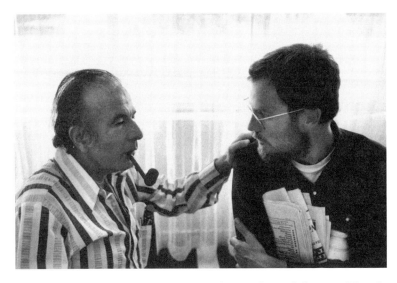

Robert Wilson is a theater innovator, playwright, and director (*Einstein on the Beach*, etc.). His theater is "cinematic," based more on images than words. The author worked in several of his pieces in the seventies. (1973)

From left to right: Marie France Pisier; the author; Isabelle Adjani; Gisela (the author's wife); François Truffaut; and an unidentified woman after *Adele H.* opening in New York in 1975.

From left to right: Sylvia (Rossellini's girlfriend); Roberto Rossellini; and Gisela (the author's wife) at author's home in New York, 1976.

François Truffaut, Alexandra Stewart (actress), and the author in New York, September 1977.

The author with director Claude Chabrol in New York, 1978.

14

What Is Mise-en-Scène?

When I stated in bygone days that everything is expressed on the screen through mise-en-scène, in no way did I intend to minimize the importance of the subject matter or the input of the many people cooperating in the making of a movie. I never intended to ignore or dismiss the significant contributions of the actors and the scriptwriters. I simply wanted to point out that the distinguishing feature of great directors lies precisely in their ability to metamorphose the stupidest plot into a meaningful work. It is obvious that if we try to summarize on paper the plot of, say, *Courage Under Fire* (directed by Edward Zwick and written by Patrick Sheane Duncan, 1996), we would end up with a very ordinary account of an investigation conducted by an officer. I don't understand how so distinguished a critic like Janet Maslin could write, "The screenwriter brazen enough to create such contrived ties between the Walden and Serling characters is Patrick Sheane Duncan, a combat veteran with a particular interest in Medal of Honor recipients. Mr Duncan's plotting is impossibly neat, but, as he demonstrated in *Mr. Holland's Opus*, he has the rare ability to shape a clichéd story in newly affecting ways."[36] Taking these remarks at face value, we are left with the impression that director Zwick's contribution consisted only in translating the script into images and Duncan is the real author of the movie! I am sure that Zwick's work on this movie, as on his other films, more closely resembled Hitchcock's collaboration with scriptwriters. As for the actors, Meg Ryan and Denzel Washington were not, in my opinion, always as convincing as they had been in other roles under the wand of different directors. Zwick succeeded in efficiently using their talent through his mise-en-scène.

What, then is mise-en-scène? This phrase, borrowed from the theater, literally means "placing on the stage." It refers to the way in which a "written play" becomes a "staged play." Can it be translated into English to mean "film direction"? Yes and no. Let me quote here from a 1970 article by Orson Welles:

> Just at this modish moment, everybody under 30—and his idiot brother—wants to be a film director. And why not? Let it be whispered that film directing (the very job itself) is often grossly overrated. Good paintings don't come from a bad painter, but good motion pictures are often signed by directors of the most perfect incompetence. Writers, editors and actors do his work for him. His only task is to speak the words "action" and "cut"—and go home with the money. Such a man can, as we have seen, wing his way through 50 years of film-directing and never be found out.[37]

Obviously, mise-en-scène and authorship in my vocabulary do not refer to such filmmakers. In the '50s and '60s in Paris, we used to call them *realisateurs* or *illustrateurs*. Perhaps comparison with literary authorship will help clarify our understanding of the notion of mise-en-scène. Jean-Paul Sartre once wrote, "One is not a writer because one has chosen to say certain things, but because one has chosen to say them *in a certain way*." This "certain way" is more than the style of the writer (author). Why should it be any different for cinema?

Let's consider the example of Brian Heap, a Jamaican story-teller who used to hold a workshop for young people in Kingston. He would read to them a "news item" about bullying. The first time, he put on a raucous dance-hall tape and roared. The adolescents, in turn, raised their fists and roared. Then Heap put on piano music and read the piece with a sympathetic, soft voice; the youngsters became subdued; some even cried. Riane Eisler, who mentions Heap's workshop in her 1995 book, called *Sacred Pleasure*, concludes that "how the stories are told can make all the difference." What the Jamaican storyteller did was mise-en-scène![38]

In our Parisian group of the '50s and '60s, we held that the "thought" of filmmakers is expressed through their mise-en-scène. Indeed, what matters in a film is the desire for order, composition, harmony, the placing of actors and objects, the choice of settings, the movements within the frame, the capturing of a gesture or a look; in short, the intellectual operation that puts an initial emotion and a general idea to work. Mise-en-scène is nothing more than the "technique" invented by author-directors to express the idea and establish the specific quality of their work. The content of the film does not matter as much as the way in which it is conveyed to the spectator. Paraphrasing Buffon's famous phrase, I would say that style makes the man— or woman.

In Paris (and elsewhere) we immediately were accused of formalism, of highlighting or upgrading form over content, form over the idea. In fact, what we were saying was simply that one cannot separate content from container. As André Malraux pointed out in one of his last literary texts, creativity resembles liquids which appear to us only through the forms they take in their containers.[39] He added that the writer's creativity (or style) lies in the interval (distance) between the actual novel and the story it is conveying. As for cinema, style is what cannot be mistaken for the subject-matter.

In any case, images have no meaning whatsoever in and of themselves. Every day, every minute, we register images that reflect our environment. They acquire significance (if any) by dint of our conventions, by the "sense" we project into them. In

other words, the image becomes meaningful through its pro-
cessing in our brains. In cinema the director-author injects meaning into the images through mise-en-scène. But the language of
cinema is not simply images as the language of literature is not
simply words. It is their *organization*, their combination by the
author that creates the meaning. This organizing process is, in
the case of cinema, mise-en-scène.

Yet, mise-en-scène is more than the visual orchestration of the
story. Speaking of the films of Nicholas Ray, Anthony Mann,
Robert Aldrich, and Richard Brooks, Jacques Rivette wrote in
1955:

> Violence is their first virtue not that facile brutality that
> made Dmytryk or Benedek successful, but a virile anger
> that comes from the heart, and is to be found less in the
> script and the plotting than in the cadences of the narrative
> and in the very technique of the mise-en-scène. And the
> frequent recourse to a discontinuous, abrupt technique
> which refuses the conventions of classical editing and con-
> tinuity is a form of "superior clumsiness" of which Cocteau
> talks, born of the need for an immediacy of expression that
> can yield, and allow the viewer to share in, the original
> emotions of the *auteur*. They are all the sons of Orson
> Welles who was the first to dare to reassert clearly an *ego-
> centric* concept of the director. The other pole of creativity
> for these (four) directors is *reflection*. Violence has no other
> purpose, once the ruins of conventions are reduced to dust,
> than to establish a void, in the midst of which, the heroes,
> completely unfettered by any arbitrary constraints, are free
> to pursue a process of self-interrogation and to delve deep
> into their destiny. That is what generates those long pauses,
> those turns that are at the centre of Ray's films, as they are
> in the films of Mann, Aldrich, and Brooks. Violence is thus
> justified by meditation, each so subtly linked to the other
> that it would be impossible to separate them without anih-
> ilating the soul of the film. This dialectic of themes re-
> appears in the terms of mise-en-scène as the dialectic of

efficacity and contemplation. (*Cahiers du Cinéma*, Christmas 1955)

Let's quote here a remark by the director of Citizen Kane, made in the last decade of his life. Decrying the new myth of the "great director," he wrote:

> Self-indulgence, the vice of all art in our epoch, is an obvious temptation to a director invested with full authority to the service of his film, and not to his own ego. Let him remain, in the best sense, the servant of his actor, not the actor's rival for attention. Above all things, let him *be loyal to the story*. The director who wants to be called the author of his film is not only responsible for the story, but *responsible to it*. (*Look*, November 3, 1970)

In this respect Douglas Sirk, who died in 1987, presents a case in point. His Hollywood credits cover more than thirty features from *Hitler's Madman* (1943), a sensationalistic saga of a Czech village destroyed by the Nazis, to the remake of *Imitation of Life* (1959), a melodramatic story of the '30s. There was no genre he did not touch and no subject he did not tackle. Indeed, one cannot find the slightest link or the remotest relation between the stories of *Thieves' Holiday* (1946), in which George Sanders plays the crook Vidocq who became Paris police prefect; *Mystery Submarine* (1950), about the destruction of a Nazi submarine in South America; *Thunder on the Hill* (1952), in which nun-sleuth Claudette Colbert establishes the innocence of a condemned woman; *The Sign of the Pagan* (1954), about Attila the Hun; *Tarnished Angels* (1958) after William Faulkner's novel; or *A Time to Love and a Time to Die* (1958), a love story set in World War II. Moreover, Sirk always worked within the framework of studio restrictions and imposed scripts. Yet his movies reveal a remarkable unity of style as well as a profoundly "poetic" temperament. How could such unity be achieved if Sirk were not a real "artist," if he had simply been loyal to the stories and a servant of his actors? (Charles Boyer's performance as a Jesuit priest in *The First Legion*, 1951, is considered his best ever; the same may also be said of Charles Coburn's role in the 1952 film *Has Anybody Seen my Gal?*) Sirk was certainly a great director, a real auteur, a master of mise-en-scène!

So was Alfred Hitchcock, the irreplacable master of suspense. His 55-year-old *Spellbound* (1945), a real gem, remains flawless despite its far-fetched story. There is not one unnecessary image or bit of dialogue in its hour and fifty-one minutes. The movie still sparkles with visual ideas, such as the camera focusing on the razor while Gregory Peck comes down the stairs toward the psychiatrist's office. And how can one forget the finale, in which the gun turns against the audience, as if everybody—all humans—were guilty! And this brings up another aspect of mise-en-scène, which involves solving problems posed by the shooting. There are many examples of problem solving in Hitchcock movies. In his 1939 lecture at Radio City Music Hall in New York, Hitchcock said, among other things:

> One advantage that the talking picture has given us is that it allowed us to delineate character a little more, through the medium of dialogue. There has been a tendency, I feel, in this development of character to rely upon the dialogue only. We have lost what has been—to me at least—the biggest enjoyment in motion pictures and that is *action and movement*. What I am trying to aim at is a combination of these two elements, character and action. The difficulty is that the two rhythms are entirely different things. I mean the rhythm and pace of action and the rhythm and pace of dialogue. The problem is to try to blend these two things together.

One can find a striking example of such a "blending" in a very difficult scene of his first American movie, shot almost immediately after his Radio City lecture. Indeed, in *Rebecca* (1940), Laurence Olivier reveals to Joan Fontaine toward the end the truth about his dead wife. He speaks for more than five minutes, which is absolutely anti-cinematic. Hitchcock found a very original cinematic treatment: When Olivier says, "She was lying on the sofa," the camera focuses on the sofa as if the scene were a flashback! He says, "She got up," and the camera moves upward. He says, "She walked toward me," and the camera pans very slowly to the left while Olivier continues to speak. He says, "She faced me," and the camera stops on a close shot of Olivier's face while he continues to speak, and so on. This was a perfect way of overcoming a script difficulty in order to visualize speech, to "blend" action and dialogue without resorting to a flashback on a character who had not been seen in the movie other than in a painting hanging on a wall! Hitchcock had brillantly solved a problem of mise-en-scène! In our reviews of the '50s, we called such finds *idées de mise-en-scène*.

Even non-auteur directors sometimes strike pay dirt. Thus, Mitchell Leisen's *Darling How Could You?* (1951) starts vividly. The camera focuses on the first page of a newspaper in which we see Theodore Roosevelt's picture and an article about Teddy's speaking before a convention. Then the camera moves backward and the enlarged frame uncovers the reader of the newspaper seated in one of the first automobiles, near a townhouse. The traffic on the avenue consists mainly of horse drawn buggies. From the house a nanny exits in a hurry, looking for a cab. This sequence lasts less than a minute and yet fills in the viewer about the epoch and some of the characters.

Another example of *idée de mise-en-scène* can be found in one of the first sequences of Rouben Mamoulian's *Dr. Jekyll and Mr. Hyde* (1932). The "subjective" camera replaces Frederic March and enters his fiancée's house, underscoring that the drama takes place *inside* the protagonist. A similar idea was used by Nicholas Ray in *Party Girl* (1958). Since it was out of question to reconstruct buildings of old Chicago, Ray took the precaution of announcing in a flamboyant caption. "Chicago in the early thirties." What do we see? A lowish-angle shot of skyscrapers painted on a backdrop with, on the left of the screen, a flashing neon suggesting the entrance of a nightclub. The camera tilts down and pans toward the neon sign. Then there is a long tracking shot closing in on the scene as if to stress even more that from now on the action of the film will take place inside the studio sets and, within them, inside the characters.

While still dealing with the opening images of great movies, let me recall John Ford's *The Searchers* (1956). In a dark room, behind a woman who slowly opens a door on sun-drenched desert scenery, the camera, as if escaping from a murky cell, shows in the distance a small cloud of dust from which emerges an approaching horse rider. Here the *idée de mise-en-scène* expresses Ford's temperatment, his love of large open spaces. In the same vein, telling the dramatic story of a locomotive engineer (after Zola's book), Jean Renoir opens *La Bête Humaine* (1938) with a train rushing toward Le Havre and shows engineer Jean Gabin and his assistant at work. Here is almost no dialogue, just beautiful shots of moving scenery. The train stops at Le Havre where we meet in a few rapid shots the other characters of the drama. This whole sequence doesn't take more than three or four minutes!

15

Pace and Rhythm

In his 1939 lecture, Hitchcock insisted on the primacy of pace and rhythm. This is indeed an essential part of what we in the '50s and '60s called mise-en-scène. In our first meeting with the Spanish director Juan Bardem (*Muerte de un Ciclista*, 1995; *Calle Mayor*, 1956; *Behind the Shutters*, 1973; etc.) in the mid-1950s, he told us that rhythm was the measure of a good movie. Without it, a film, no matter how well conceived and played, would be a failure. Curiously enough, he seemed to attribute a successful "rhythm" to chance! Many directors refer to "rhythm" as some sort of a "mysterious" ingredient which might appear (or not) after the completion of the movie. In any case, in the absence of rhythm, movies seem verbose. Facing a lack of rhythm, directors try to compensate through editing, music, added commentary, and the like. To Hitchcock, as he explained in his 1939 lecture, it is up to the director to create it: "I think that pace in a film is made entirely by keeping the mind of the spectator occupied. You don't need to have quick cutting, you don't need to have quick playing, but you do need a very full story and the changing of one situation to another. You need the changing of one incident to another, so that all the time the audience's mind is occupied." He referred to the tendency in modern novels and stage plays to abandon story in favor of characterization and psychology. Motion pictures, he added, need "quite an amount of story." By way of explanation, he said that, after an hour, the audience starts to get tired and needs "the injection of some dope" to keep them occupied mentally. "As long as you can sustain that and not let up, you have pace. That is why suspense is such a valuable thing." It seems that Hitchcock equates suspense with rhythm. Let me quote again from his 1939 lecture:

> You must design your incidents and your story shape to mount up. I always think the film shape is very much like the short story. Once it starts, you haven't time to let up. You must go through and your film must end on its highest note. It must never go over the curve. Once you have reached your high spot, then the film is stopped. Now one of the things that is going to help you hold all these things together and provide you that shape is the suspense. Suspense, I feel, is a very important factor in nearly all motion pictures. It can be arrived at in many different ways. To me there is no argument that a surprise lasting about ten seconds, however painful, is not half as good as suspense for about six or seven reels. I think that nearly all stories can do with suspense. Even a love story can have it. We used to feel that suspense was saving someone from the scaffold, or something like that, but there is also the suspense of whether the man will get the girl. I really feel that suspense has to do largely with the audience's own desire or wishes.

Hitchcock distinguished between two types of suspense—*objective* and *subjective*. Objective suspense is of the "chase" type: Viewers see it directly on the screen. Subjective suspense, by contrast, lets the audience experience it through the eyes or mind of one of the characters. Of this type, he said: "Instead of doing it, say as Griffith used to do, by cutting to the galloping feet of the horse and then going to the scaffold, instead of showing both sides, I like to show only one side. In the French Revolution, probably, someone said to Danton, 'Will you please hurry on your horse,' but never show him getting on the horse. Let the audience worry whether the horse has even started. That is making the audience play its part."

In most recent action-packed movies, directors use both types. It sometimes amounts to what I would call a kind of "mechanically" propelled suspense, as seen, for example, in the *Die Hard* films. While watching such movies, spectators remain glued to the screen, but once the movie stops, they forget it. With directors like Wolfgang Petersen (*Air Force One*, for instance), the effect is more subtle and many scenes linger in the mind of viewers long after they leave the theater.

Let me quote a remark that the Franco-American writer Julien Green made in his diary (August 29, 1947) about a dream he had the night before: "This dream was more real, more intense than real life, because only what could serve the action was highlighted. That confirms for me that the man who dreams is sometimes a more gifted artist than the man fully awake." Highlighting what "serves the action"—is this not the basis of pace and rhythm? Moreover, this comment by Green underscores the link between cinema and dreams!

Rhythm and pace are masterfully introduced in the re-edit of *Touch of Evil* (1998). The suspense was already present in the 1958 release despite the editing by Universal Studios. Once again, Orson Welles proved his great directorial and acting talents. The three-minute, no-cut, opening track shot remains unmatched in film history: It superbly defines the characters and their environment and sets the pace. Camera movements become part of the story and convey the suspense while details about the characters' inner lives come to the fore. Every shot brilliantly illustrates Welles's directorial work both on the level of rhythm and what we used to call *idées de mise-en-scène*. Even in the original studio release, against Welles's own plan, it was a great movie. The director's presence is felt all along and the movie proves how an auteur can transform the stupidest script into a masterpiece of art! As one critic noted, "The camera itself is almost a character."[40]

16

Light as a Character

Ingmar Bergman's director of photography, Sven Nykvist, once said to Richard Eder, "There are people in a room. The sunlight comes into the room. It walks across the room. When it does, the people stop talking. When the light walks, something is happening." Some directors leave the lighting to the cinematographer. Others consider it an expressive element and discuss how to use it with the cameraman. Bergman belongs to the latter group, for whom light is not only an event but almost a character. As Eder wrote, Bergman's actors react to light as if it were another actor speaking to them. In *Face to Face* (1975), for instance, the lighting of the grandparents' home shifted subtly when it became part of Liv Ullmann's dreams. In *Wild Strawberries* (1957), too, changes in lighting enhance the differences between the present and memories of the past. Liv Ullman recalled, "Light shows you what to do. You don't act the same way when it changes." Bergman works intimately with his cameraman Nykvist, explaining what kind of light he wants. For the dream in *Face to Face* he penciled the words "a flowing light"; for the dream and memory scenes in Strawberries, "plain, full light." Nykvist takes these notions and translates them into lighting. He told Eder that during the preparation of *Winter Light* (1962) there was a scene covering a period of three hours in a church. He assumed that a single light setting would be enough. Bergman took him to the church and they sat for three hours. Every five minutes he had to take a photograph. "I realized how all these tiny shifts of light worked out into what Bergman was trying to do" (*New York Times,* April 7, 1976).

The French cinematographer Henri Alekan, who worked with such directors as Jean Cocteau (*La Belle et la Bête,* 1946) and Abel Gance (*Austerlitz,* 1960) and achieved fame on his own, used to complain about the so-called New Wave films: "Their lighting recalls one of aquariums." Joseph Losey called him the "absolute perfectionist." In Alekan's opinion, lighting is not only a technical problem, it is also "visual music" that impacts both space and action" (*Le Monde* July 30–31, 1988). In the United States, Greg Toland was considered one of the greatest cinematographers ever by both William Wyler and Orson Welles. With his lighting, he created just the right atmosphere for each sequence.

I do not think it necessary to elaborate further on lighting as part of the mise-en-scène. After all, from that angle, filmmakers have learned from great painters. Thus the lighting in Jean Renoir's *Le Déjeuner sur L'Herbe* (1959) reminds one of his father's canvases!

17

Settings and Details

The choice and arrangement of the settings are also part of the mise-en-scène, inasmuch as they convey meanings to the audience. As an example, I refer to Kubrick's *Paths of Glory* (1957) and more particularly to the sequence in which a French company commander (Kirk Douglas) pleads with the general (Adolphe Menjou) for the lives of three soldiers condemned to death for cowardice. Just before this scene, Kubrick shows horrifying pictures of men in trenches under rain and enemy firing. Suddenly the film jumps from the mud to the snowy marble of a chateau's huge gilt and brocade salon filled with spindle-legged chairs, crystal chandeliers, and porcelain cherubs. The mud-covered colonel confronts the nattily dressed and well-spoken general who is eating a gourmet lunch and drinking with gusto a rare Bordeaux. The contrast speaks for itself with little dialogue, and the details of the setting make it obvious that Menjou will not yield.

To be sure, viewers do not register or notice all the details of the settings. They retain an overall impression but are conscious of few details. The art of the director consists, in part, of stirring up the audience's curiosity and inducing spectators into becoming detectives. Details scattered by the director in the frame are indeed clues containing parts of the overall meaning of the story and its characters. Just as Sherlock Holmes would unravel a mystery through the study of numerous footprints, differences in mud, cigarette ashes, and the like, moviegoers must understand and appreciate a film through all that they see on the screen, including the accumulated details in the settings. Like a master's canvas, a good film provides hidden meanings behind its apparent display. After the release of *2001*, Kubrick gave the following answer to a journalist seeking hidden meaning in the film: "How could we possibly appreciate the *Mona Lisa* if Leonardo had written at the bottom of the canvas, 'The lady is smiling because she is hiding a secret from her lover.' This would shackle the viewer to reality, and I don't want this to happen to *2001*."

Facial reactions by protagonists shown in close-ups are assimilated with telling details. I would like to add here another remark by Stanley Kubrick: "In terms of working with actors, a director's job more closely resembles that of a novelist than of a Svengali. One assumes that one hires actors who are great virtuosos. It is too late to start running an acting class in front of the cameras, and essentially what the director must do is to provide the right ideas for the scene, the right adverb, the right adjective" (interview with Bernard Weinraub in the *New York Times*, January 4, 1972).

I hope that the foregoing remarks have helped in clarifying the concept of mise-en-scène as we used it in our articles in the '50s and '60s. Let me repeat that it may be defined as the technique by which all great directors convey their style, their world. Obviously, style varies from one director to another. It also varies with time. Today's movies are different from those of the '60s and '70s, just as those were different from their predecessors in the '30s and '40s. It is as if generational changes were affecting the cinema world every twenty years or so. Or is it because of the buildup of sunspots at approximately fifteen-year intervals? (Contemporary scientists have demonstrated links between these solar variations and disturbances in our climate. Indeed, sunspots affect the human metabolism; filmmakers, being humans are therefore subject to this solar phenomenon!)

18

Changes in Filmmaking in the '60s and '70s

To be sure, advances in communications technology bring about changes in the ways in which films are conceived and produced. For instance, the advent of sound in the late '20s erased the agonized performances of the silent-era actors as well as the innumerable close-ups and excessive make-up. All of a sudden, films looked very different! Later, the systematic use of color suppressed at least for some time the plethora of contrasted images. But these changes were negligible compared to those prompted by contemporary technological leaps, such as today's digitally designed images.

Since the end of the last world war, two important crises hit the world of cinema. The first one, in the '50s, was mainly attributed to the spread of television. Between 1947 and 1957, attendance at movie theaters dwindled in the United States from 95 million to 45 million. Experts affirm that most of the lost audience turned to television. Though it is true that the small screen attracted millions, other factors played a more important role in the decline in moviegoing. Indeed, the 1960s witnessed important societal changes. There was a kind of "maturation" of the public: People demanded "adult" pictures. They were fed up with movies that were made to appeal to the lowest common denominator. Hollywood's "code" was bursting at the seams. Even kids shun yarns designed just for them. This was not a passing fad. Rather, it reflected a profound shift in the tastes and perceptions of all age groups and social classes, brought by World War II and the spread of education and information (compounded by the development of television). At any rate, the scope of public disaffection dismayed the film industry. Corporate executives, market specialists, sociologists, economists, journalists, producers, and directors searched for causes.

The venerable "intellectual" magazine of those days, *Saturday Review*, devoted most of its December 19, 1959 issue to what it called "unrest in the motion-picture industry, not only in Hollywood but throughout the film-producing world." The editorial, signed by Arthur Knight, noted that

> New themes, new trends, new names have flashed across our screens during the past year.... In America, filmmakers, with greater independence than they have ever known, are fevereshly blending together new ingredients ... "Maturity" has suddenly become a fetish. The soundtracks carry dialogue that would have been unthinkable as little as a year ago; the scripts contain situations hitherto expressly forbidden. In England, France, Germany and Poland, young directors are smashing the conventions ... The revolution is posing new problems for the studios.

The *revolution*! In fact, the movement had started in the early 1950s in Paris with a bunch of film fans who fought against the French "filmic establishment" in two obscure and recently founded magazines, the leftist *Positif* and the apolitical *Cahiers du Cinéma*. I became part of this turmoil because it happened that I was in Paris at the right time and met the right people! The objective of our group of activists was threefold: to enhance the "art" component of the film industry; to reduce the cost of filmmaking; and to open the gates to young directors and encourage them to produce "personal" movies. Thanks to

Truffaut's talent and pugnacity, *Cahiers*'s group gained a wide international audience and many of its members were able to make films as early as 1958. This movement came to be known as the French New Wave. It naturally triggered similar developments elsewhere in Europe before reaching U.S. East Coast and inspiring film critics such as Andrew Sarris and independent filmmakers. In retrospect, I believe that our keen interest in Hollywood's B-movies stirred curiosity in the United States and propelled the spread of our ideas.

In the above-mentioned issue of *Saturday Review*, William Fadiman who was at the time executive story director of the Columbia Pictures Corporation, mentioned some of the problems facing the industry in the United States: rising production costs; the need to cater to America's own evolving cultural standards; the shifting tastes in entertainment; competition with television. Curiously enough, the author of the article counted books among the "doughty" rivals of the film industry for "America's leisure-time dollar." Consider this: 2,200 fiction titles were published in 1958 in the United States. "Again and again," wrote Fadiman, "books which are not remotely 'entertaining' in the conventional, undemanding sense have been enthusiastically received, enthusiastically read and enthusiastically catapulted onto the best-sellers lists." Moreover, many books that did not achieve wide popularity "were applauded for their high quality" and "there are more books and plays evidencing discrimination and quality than there are films in proportionate numbers. The Academy Awards which crown filmdom's highest achievements cannot be equated, in terms of literacy, with the Pulitzer Prizes awarded books and plays."

In Fadiman's view, basic changes were taking place in Hollywood:

We have only recently been released from the obligation to make films according to formulas evolved by the heads of the seven major studios. There is no longer an MGM brand, a Paramount style, a Columbia pattern. Both in the corporate and practical sense, major studios have either vanished or will do so shortly. They have been replaced by independent producers who function without adherence to the mandates of a giant parent company. This is a huge step forward. . . . We must be imaginative, different, stimulating, adult. We must sow and cultivate our garden of talent.

In the words of another contributor to *Saturday Review*, Arthur Knight, as long as production costs continue to spiral, original stories, scripts written directly for the screen, directors with picture ideas of their own will remain "anomalies." He concluded his article with these lines: "There is a new frankness in films, a new maturity. But the industry still has a lot of growing up to do."

Another contributor to *Saturday Review*'s special issue, Hollis Alpert, wrote, "Frank Sinatra can make any kind of movie he wants to at any time, but some bright fellow with an idea and a genuine urge to do something different hasn't a prayer. The French have found a way. They aren't wrong, and let's hope they keep it up." But as I indicated earlier, the promises of the New Wave were short-lived. Most of the young directors turned toward the industry and gradually became part of it. Chabrol rapidly became less interested in quality than quantity. Truffaut forgot about unknown players and embraced stars. Most of the young directors produced clumsily made movies. Some surrendered to cheap sensationalism and commercialism, if not pornography. (One wonders what would have become of Vadim's *Et Dieu Créa la Femme*, without Brigitte Bardot's unveiled charms?) With the turmoils of the late '60s, Godard turned to "political" cinema devoid of any artistic value whatsoever.

The unrest in the motion picture industry, signaled in the December 1959 issue of *Saturday Review*, reached a peak in the early 1970s. When I arrived in New York in 1971, Lillian Hellman—who had heard about my book on detective novels in which I had praised her companion, Dashiell Hammet—invited me to her place together with some New York intellectuals. At her party I met Renata Adler who at that time used to write about films for the *New York Times*. Naturally, we had a discussion about cinema. Lillian told me, "Here too films are changing. Movies are now interesting more and more intelligent people, at any rate more than the stage." Everybody had a word on the reasons for the "crisis" that was hitting Hollywood. But after a while I noticed that I shared neither Hellman's nor Adler's opinions on films. So I diplomatically (I had become an ambassador to the United Nations!) changed the subject and spoke about my other interests. In a corner of Lillian's bookcase I found a 1970 (November 3) *Look* magazine special issue on "The New Hollywood." I asked to borrow it. Lillian said, "You may keep it."

Jack Hamilton, senior editor, opened the magazine with these words:

> The movies, America's favorite and most enduring entertainment, take over this entire issue of *Look*. In a widly changing world, Hollywood has been forced to make some sense out of its irrelevant, ostrich-like production Code and begin to look at things the way they really are. Even Bob Hope of the Old Guard said on Academy Award night: "Never again will Hollywood be accused of showing a lollipop world. They have fearlessly, and for the most part with excellent taste, examined behavior long considered taboo." We think that movies today are more alive, more filled with surprises, more talked about than ever. The irony is that Hollywood has become an economic disaster area just when the movies are beginning to look up. But does the death of the formula studio system really matter? The new movies are made all over America by all kinds of Americans.

Yet, in 1970, the industry suffered heavy losses especially on overblown budgets for some ill-fated epics. Debt-loaded studios auctioned off the "adornments" of their stars, their accumulated furniture and other accessories, their real-estate holdings, their stockpile movies. Why? A contributor to the special issue, Fletcher Knebel, diagnosed the cause as follows:

> You see, the biggies had it all wrong. They kept making those grand spectacles for umpteen millions, like *Hello Dolly, Sweet Charity* and *Doctor Dolittle*, at a time when you and I, the flick audience, were undergoing a crisis of values, right? and searching for our identity, and suffering hot anti-Establishment flashes. What we wanted from that big, wide screen was something that involved us personally like that Fonda kid on a star-spangled motorcycle, cruising around, making it with broads, smoking grass and trying to keep those hick pigs off his back long enough so he could figure out who he was.

Indeed, the late '60s and early '70s were the years of student turmoil all over the Western world, the years of the hippies in the United States, the years of the Black Panthers, of the Vietnam war, of the civil rights marches, of Manson's group savagely killing Sharon Tate and her guests, and so on. In 1970, the feature-length documentary on the 1969 *Woodstock* rock festival became the biggest hit of the year in many countries. David Picker, president of United Artists declared, "This is a great day for creators, for those with new ideas, for people whose first love is making good movies" Forty percent of 1970s American movies were produced by independents, including *M*A*S*H, Five Easy Pieces, Carnal Knowledge, Mean Streets, Husbands,* and many others. Audiences increasingly regarded movies as an art form, but almost half of American moviegoers were between 16 and 24 years of age according to the Motion Picture Association. So a lot of movies were made to cater to their tastes. But the other half of the audience was not captivated by the so-called "youth" products. "Adult" and "family" pictures actually brought in more money at the box office. In 1969, for instance, *Midnight Cowboy* (an alienated-youth yarn) yielded $11 million at the box office. But six "non-youth" movies grossed more that same year: *The Love*

Bug, Funny Girl, Bullit, Butch Cassidy and the Sundance Kid, Romeo and Juliet, and *True Grit.*

The "revolution" was more in the headlines than in the field! Television continued to gnaw away at the movie-audience pie. Between 1958 and 1969, according to *Look*'s special issue, movie box-office grosses suffered a 45 percent decline! Nevertheless, during the same period fundamental changes appeared in moviemaking. Indeed, the tastes of the moviegoing public had changed in fundamental ways because of the development of the information media. With the spread of radio and television, we now live in an age of mass communications, easy and cheap travel. Every day more and more people explore the world and learn about it. Technology has speeded up daily routines and the perceived acceleration of time is steadily intensifying. This is an age of intercommunications. This is an age of mutual influencing and learning. The public is alert. This is an age of awakening, not of slumbering. Or is it?

I cannot leave this section without a word about the videocassette "revolution." Up to the 1970s, pro-Gutenberg activists touted the superior advantages of books, their easy access and storage. One could keep the book in a private library, consult it at any moment, earmark one paragraph, leave it, come back to it. This seems very difficult if not impossible with films; even if you find the desired movie, you needs a projector and must go through almost all of it to find the scene in which you are interested. This certainly was a problem. I say *was*, because technology finally overcame this difficulty through what was called in the early 1970s the videocassette revolution (yet another revolution! I fear that by using the word "revolution" so often we are making it hackneyed. Any new invention in the field of electronic communications profoundly changes our environment and our desires).

In any case, the first videocassette recorders hit the American market almost at the same time as I arrived in New York. I bought one. It was a heavy and complicated contraption, manufactured by Sony, and it used large tapes. It could tape any one-hour program for delayed screening. A year or so later, CBS designed a more sophisticated model built by Motorola. It was still expensive and its cartridges could record either fifty minutes of black and white or twenty-five minutes of color. By the mid-'70s, cheaper and handier recorders became available. By the end of the '70s, videocassette recorders and videodisc players underwent a kind of metamorphosis. Together with the combination of cable TV, earth stations, and satellites, the new technologies multiplied the channels and opened the way to a variety of new networks and new businesses. After thirty or forty years of serving as the provider of a limited number of mass audience entertainment and news programs, television opened itself to all sorts of specialized and niche programming. All this posed a serious challenge to the established networks, forcing them to enter the fields of cable and video. On the individual level, you can now keep a film library at home, rent almost any movie from video stores, play back all or part of films, and more. This gave rise to a whole new branch of filmmaking: features as well as shorts taped directly and shown on television or elsewhere.

19

Changes in Filmmaking in the '80s and '90s

Changes in filmmaking continued at a more or less rapid pace in the '80s and '90s. To a large extent, they were the continuation of the trends that had appeared during the previous two decades. With the old studio system almost completely dismantled, the directors became the sole masters aboard their ships, controlling everything from the scripts and the actors to the editors and distributors. In the bygone days, directors generally had to respect the 90-minute length necessary for theater owners to sell popcorn and candy during the intermissions. That forced directors to find ways to convey their story quickly. They had to imagine and invent "niceties" (what we, in Paris, called *idées de mise-en-scène*) as I described earlier. Now, television had absorbed newsreels and shorts and there were no more intermissions: Patrons would buy their popcorn at the start of the show and still expect a two-hour entertainment for the price of their ticket! Therefore, features had to last about 120 minutes instead of the average 90 minutes of the past.

With an extra thirty minutes and without studio control, directors felt free to tell their stories as they wished. At the same time, unions had gained recognition for the contributions of their members. Thus, the credits became much longer. In the old days, the credits were extremely short. Except for the producer, the director, and, sometimes, the scriptwriter, the names of the technicians were compressed into two or three frames. Today, each participant has his own solo panel no matter how scanty his or her contribution! No more compression of names: Those who don't find themselves listed at the start appear at the end, together with musical accompaniment! Moreover, in the past, credits were occasionally created by well-known animation artists whose contribution, although unrelated to the subject of the movie, delighted the audience for one or two minutes. This trend, which resulted in the addition of a creative artist on top of the director, seems to have faded completely.

At any rate, the change in new movies goes beyond the credits! As I just indicated, directorial "niceties" show up less frequently in contemporary movies, in which superfluous dialogue, pompously dubbed "adult language," and repetitious images often dull more than one scene. In many cases, directors rely on rowdy, loud, and disruptive special effects and high-pitched sound tracks to impress the audience and suspend its disbelief. Otherwise, movies such as the *Die Hards* or the *Terminators* are well edited and entertaining. The violence they display reflects a general trend: Today's films border on ferocity if not outright viciousness compared to those of only a decade ago. Watching such martial arts exhibitions as those in Steven Segal's *Under Siege* and other similar productions, one wonders how the characters are supposed to survive so many wicked blows! Unrealistic? Sure, but who cares? Fury and rage pervade all entertainment products, even those intended for children. This is a societal problem that falls outside the scope of this book.

The rub, if any, is that extreme violence doesn't replace "meaning." Even in the case of self-conscious filmmakers whose work echoes that of "masters" of the past, something is missing. Let's take, for instance, the films of shrewd and talented directors like Brian DePalma or Andrew Davis who do not hide their profound admiration for Alfred Hitchcock. DePalma is already an old hand, as he started his career in the 1960s. His 1981 *Dressed to Kill* exemplifies his best work: technical virtuosity, constant nerve tickling, masterful use of camera movements combined with a skillful sound track. The inclusion of a "shower scene" constitutes a direct homage to Hitchcock's *Psycho* (1960). As in the case of the "master of suspense," DePalma's camera is insistently "voyeuristic." But, instead of showing intercourse, per se, Hitchcock introduced the "cycle of love making," so to speak, in the very structure of his films. Indeed, his kind of suspense followed the pattern of "sex": foreplay, gradual build-up of excitation, climax, decrease of tension. That's why he could avoid love-making scenes and yet insert multiple erotic "touches." (For instance, in his 1954 *Rear Window* eroticism is concentrated in a rapid shot of Grace Kelly extracting a nightgown from her small suitcase and in some of the neighbor's actions that Jimmy Stewart watches through his magnifying lens.) DePalma, by contrast, often takes his protagonists to bed, interrupting the suspense each time. Thus, erotic voyeurism pervades *Body Double* (1984) to such an extent that viewers tend to forget the story line!

To further illustrate this shift, consider recent e-mail from a friend of mine, Brent Brolin (an architect):

I was watching an old Cary Grant movie last weekend and was reminded of what you always say about the movies as a (subtle) visual medium vis à vis the huffing the puffing sex scenes that have become obligatory nowadays. Grant had gone into a record store because he spied an attractive salesgirl there (Irene Dunne). He bought a huge pile of records and, as it was the end of the day, managed to walk along with her as she went home. When she stopped, saying this was her house, he paused (still carrying a huge pile of records), picked one off the top and held it out saying, "Can I hear this on your victrola?" She asked if he had a record player. He said no. And she, with barely a hint of coyness, reached out for the record, slowly (but not too slowly) drew it out of its paper slip case, turned and walked up the stairs to the doorway, lovely, delicate and very sexy. The next day we saw *Random Hearts* and were

treated to lots of skin and sweat but nothing so erotic as a
record being taken out of its case. (November 1, 1999)

In the same vein as DePalma, Andrew Davis's *The Fugitive*
(1994) illustrates some of the new trends in filmmaking. The
movie works smoothly and efficiently, like a well-oiled engine.
As in Hitchcock's *The Wrong Man* (1957), the lead character, Harrison Ford, is falsely accused. But unlike Henry Fonda in Hitchcock's film, Ford escapes and is pursued by federal agent
Tommy Lee Jones. The movie is suspensefully constructed.
Viewers remain glued to the screen until the end. Solid script,
good acting, efficient direction. But as in DePalma's movies—
but not Hitchcock's—once the film is over, it does not *haunt* the
spectator, who rapidly forgets the plot and Harrison Ford's pre-
dicament. I vividly remember that days after having seen *The
Wrong Man*, many scenes continued to linger in my head. I often
thought of the tragedy caused by the inaccurate testimony of the
three female bank employees. In short, there was a "meaning"
(something more than the apparent story) in Hitchcock's movie,
which was missing in Davis's. The old master insisted on the
personal side of his characters, beefed them up. In contemporary
thrillers, characters are sketchy; their personal lives are described
perfunctorily or only alluded to. Who, for instance, remembers
Bruce Willis's family ties in the first *Die Hard* (1988)?

In most of today's films, substance is to be found in dialogue,
not in images. Thus, for instance, in *The Fugitive* Tommy Lee
Jones *says* that Ford's innocence or culpability doesn't interest
him; he is paid to pursue and capture a fugitive. To DePalma,
Ted Kennedy's Chappaquiddick tragedy is only a pretext for
technical prowess and thriller-like narration (*Blow Out*, 1981); a
few "substantive" allusions make some dialogue lines sparkle.
Generally speaking, dialogue reigns supreme in today's cinema.
I still remember my thoughts after seeing *St. Elmo's Fire* (1985):
The greatest part of the story, as well as the evolution of the
characters (students who just graduated from college), was concentrated in the dialogue. At first sight, it looked as if the script

had been adapted from a stage play. The director, Joel Schumacher (who directed *Batman* in 1997) had forgotten that image was the "language" of film. I am not suggesting a return to the silents. I am merely saying that the unfolding of the story should not be confined to the dialogue! A similar remark can be made about Godard. He often does not rely essentially on images; rather, he uses a lot of dialogue and commentaries, concealing them behind his "hectic" editing. But editing, like special effects, is closer to tricks than to cinematic language!

I doubt that Schumacher was under Godard's spell while shooting *St. Elmo*. The invasion of dialogue is certainly due, at least in part, to TV (the small screen does not allow the viewer to pick up subtle facial expressions or details of the settings as well as the silver screen). Moreover, because the script was essentially a "literary" work, the writers naturally relied on dialogue more than images. Hence the tendency to forget that cinema is first and foremost based on images. Elia Kazan recalls in his memoirs that John Ford used to advise him to shoot his movies as if they were silents. And, to test the accuracy of his films, Joseph Losey used to show them to a selected audience without the sound track! I personally saw Mizogushi's *The 36 Ronins* without subtitles and still understood what was happening on the screen! Today, dialogue, sound, and "tricks" tend to replace mise-en-scène. Would *Jurassic Park* or *Titanic* have been box-office hits without their expensive special effects and "smashing" sound tracks? Musing about the rapid decline of the New Wave directors (including himself) at the box office, my friend François Truffaut once said that cinema was, in fact, closer to the circus than any other form of entertainment.

Joel Schumacher acknowledges a change in filmmaking. In his opinion, reported by Bernard Weinraub (*New York Times*, June 9, 1997): "There are no rules now, and that's great. There used to be the tried and true way: You got a bestseller, two big movie stars and an A-list director and you had a hit. That's not true anymore. Three teen-agers making a film in a garage can win the Academy Award. Anything goes. Studios will take a chance on someone brand new. But, the trouble is, directors get gobbled, like celebrities. If you're hot, it's great. The salaries are astronomical. If there's no hot on you, you don't exist." Weinraub, who interviewed many producers, directors, studio executives, and the like, sees a quiet *generational shift*, a *new wave* of directors whose artistic sensibility and "flashy" editing style seem very different from the filmmakers of the '70s and '80s. He attributes this shift to the changing tastes of the audiences. The new directors have attracted diverse audiences. Weinraub classifies them as follows: At one end of his scale are somewhat arty filmmakers, such as Anthony Minghella (*The English Patient*); Danny Boyle (*Trainspotting*); and Scott Hicks (*Shine*). One member of this group, the Australian Baz Luhrmann (*Strictly Ballroom*), says that people are moving toward a different way of seeing and listening to things. At the opposite end of his scale, Weinraub puts commercial directors like Michael Bay (*Bad Boys*), whose "jagged style" reflects the world of MTV and slick Television commercials. Bay told Weinraub, "What we're seeing now in movies is constant bombardment and visual stimulus: things are now faster and bigger; sounds are louder." Many movies are built on natural (or unnatural) catastrophes. But they sustain the attention of the viewer only through artifice. In this connection, I would like to remind their directors (and scriptwriters) of the famous Cecil B. DeMille phrase. "I want a story that starts with an earthquake and works up to a climax"!

True, not all directors follow the new trends. Some of the most successful remain loyal to clarity. Edward Zwick (*Legends of the Fall, Glory, Courage Under Fire*) confided to Stephen Hunter of the *Washington Post* (November 8, 1998), "I believe in the fundamental precepts of storytelling. I have a commitment to the tradition of classical drama." He still tells stories with a beginning, a middle, and an end! "Every artist," he added, "is concerned about staying current and worries about losing the popular audience. But maybe you cannot anticipate that. Look at *Legends of the Fall*. It was the most conventional 'old movie' but it was also the most popular!" In an article titled "Making Hollywood Movies by the

Numbers" (*New York Times*, January 12, 1997) he himself wrote about the '60s and '70s movies such as *Bonnie and Clyde* (Arthur Penn), *Carnal Knowledge* (Mike Nichols), *Klute* (Alan J. Pakula), *M*A*S*H* (Robert Altman), *The Conversation* (Francis Ford Coppola) and some others: "These were the films that left my generation weeping in the darkness or sent us flying out of the theater and back into the dorm for hour upon hour of cigarette-hazed conversation. They challenged us to look at our lives, at our politics, at our society, to look inward and to open our most secret heart." Zwick defines the changes in the following terms: "The stakes have grown so high. With each film a start-up business of $50 to $100 million succeeds or fails in a single weekend." This situation has pushed everybody, including the directors he admired so much in his student days, to share "another common bond": making movies based on the same kind of "high-concept" bestseller whose most distinctive quality seems to be the guarantee of a strong opening weekend. Today there are only two kinds of movies in Hollywood: hits or flops. He concluded his article by saying, "We end up with movies that appear to have been made by the numbers. I am still idealistic enough to believe that time, not box office, will be the final arbiter."

On the producer's side, Bernard Weinraub quoted Scott Rudin in his above-mentioned report: "There is a changing of the guard. Some extremely gifted filmmakers of the '70s and '80s are having a hard time right now because the audience is getting conditioned to an overheated style of moviemaking." Another producer interviewed by Weinraub contended that such changes happen every ten to fifteen years (the change cycle of sunspots, as I indicated earlier!).

Since the invention of the camera, moviemaking has undergone many changes. These were sometimes due to technological advances (sound, color, television, wide screens, multi-focal "zoom" lenses, etc). Some important changes were caused by the spread of information and education since World War II. Indeed, audiences have become more selective. The new technologies are also having a deep impact on moviemaking. In addition, during the past two decades there has been a trend toward longer movies: two hours and more, often without any real justification (Erich Von Stroheim, who was regarded as insane when he filmed *Greed* in 1924 in a ten-hour-long version, is vindicated!). Maureen Dowd, a *New York Times* columnist, has also noticed a change in acting (July 5, 1997). She recalled in her op-ed piece Robert Mitchum and Jimmy Stewart: "What was really striking about these two men was how proudly *un*mythical they were. They lived in a time, unthinkable today, when celebrity was not the enemy of modesty." She goes on to say: "In today's Hollywood, anyone with star potential wants to stretch. Why must Kevin Costner inflict on the viewer a bad English accent in *Robin Hood*? Why would we want to see Michelle Pfeifer play a pallid wallflower in *Frankie and Johnny*? Why would we want to see Julia Roberts with shaved eyebrows in *Mary Reilly*? We live in an age without limits now, and so the junk that Hollywood turns out is limitless."

One veteran actor has some strong opinions on the changes in film producing and making as well. In June 1997 in Pittsburgh for his one-man show, Gregory Peck made no bones about criticizing the new movies. James Hirsh of the *Wall Street Journal* (June 18, 1997) reported his diatribe as follows: "Mr. Peck clearly misses the old days. He blasts the corporate-run studios of today for focusing more on profit than creativity, deriding their works as 'conglomorate films.' Their gratuitous violence and graphic sex make him bristle. He prefers independent films, citing *Sling Blade* and *Secrets and Lies*."

So, whatever the reasons, films are changing. Looking at the present state of film production in Hollywood, I would say that, in general, what essentially distinguishes new films from old ones is the way stories are told. Linear storytelling has largely given way to a more *hectic tempo*. Sometimes, as a result of this style of narration, the story loses all clarity whatsoever and becomes incomprehensible as, for instance, in *Mission Impossible* (1997). In my opinion, the changes we are now witnessing are largely linked to the development of new technologies (digital, for instance) that have completely transformed the special effects realm. Moreover, a number of films targeted toward teenagers, recall the '50s and '60s movies about youth. To take one example, the subject of *Reality Bites* (Ben Stiller, 1993) is not far removed from that of *Rebel Without a Cause* (Nicholas Ray, 1955): Both aspire to describe the confusion and aimlessness of youth. But what a difference in style! Ray was already a middle-aged director with a number of great movies behind him when he made *Rebel*, while Stiller at age 28 was just starting his career. Furthermore, Stiller was obviously raised on TV rather than on movies.

In more recent films, the influence of TV sitcoms and music videos is quite clear. Dialogue recalls TV shows' one-liners or even commercial slogans! As for images and editing, the word that comes to mind is *jumping*; jumping from one angle to another, from one scene to another! The same discontinuity (a word I use for want of a better one) is also apparent in movies aimed at adult or general audiences. It is often said that my colleague at *Cahiers du Cinéma*, Jean-Luc Godard, invented that style of narration, in his special way of editing. In fact, he used it in *À Bout de Souffle* (*Breathless*, 1959) because his producer was short of money and could not pay for extra filming. Besides, nobody can pretend to have "invented" discontinuity in narration. Indeed, in our nightly dreams, discontinuity has always been— and still is—the rule! Indeed, dreams are full of uncertainties and jumps in plot, location, characters, and objects.

20

Cinema and Television

The new trends in filmmaking are due to many causes, among them the rapid development of television. I have already mentioned, in passing, the influence of the small screen on filmmaking. I would now like to expand on this subject.

It is often said that television is the extension of cinema, as it is essentially a visual contraption that brings the movies in the sitting room. At first glance, this assessment seems obvious. But, in reality, things are not as simple as they appear. While it is evident that the TV screen presents an image, very often this image is one of a man or a woman talking to the host of a show or directly to the viewer, as in news programs. Actually, because of copyright problems, television, in its beginnings, transmitted more news and talk shows than movies. It looked more like an extension of radio, like a radio in which the listener would see the image of the speaker. Yet, it has had a deep impact on individuals and societies, which, in turn, have influenced people's tastes and all of show business. Over the years, many studies and panel discussions have been devoted to the effects of this medium, which was initially dubbed by some as the plug-in drug. Indeed, TV instills an attitude of passive withdrawal from direct involvement in life. Some experts say that it diminishes individual creativity. I remember that in the mid-1970s (or was it a little later?) the University of Berlin and one of the German TV channels conducted a study of two working-class families that abstained from watching TV for four weeks. No definite conclusions were reached and the families resumed their viewing and watched TV even more than before! According to George W. S. Trow, author of *My Pilgrim's Progress: Media Studies, 1950–1998* (New York, 1999), television has thrown off the way Americans construe their world; its rhythms and tropes have infused and corroded all aspects and expressions of culture; the very ways we think and feel have been transformed under the influence of the "bluish glow of the box." If such an assessment is correct one has to conclude that television has had an indirect impact on filmmakers, since, as children, today's directors and scriptwriters were TV addicts or, at the very least, largely exposed to TV.

In order to uncover the influence of the new medium on cinema, we must also explore the differences between them First and foremost, TV images are not as clear as those displayed on the silver screen. Even the highly publicized, incipient high-definition television (HDTV) doesn't approach the sharpness of the film image. Moreover, the very smallness of the screen erases important details. For instance, Jack Nicholson, swaggering in canary yellow (*Prizzi's Honor*, John Huston, 1985) does not have the same effect on a forty- or even a fifty-inch screen as on a thirty-foot one. In addition, movies (directly shown on TV or through videos) look very different at home, not only because of the screen's size, but also because of the environment; indeed, viewing them amid large audiences somehow changes one's perception. Psychological factors are at play here. For instance, a spectator interviewed by a reporter admitted, "A lot of times funny movies are just funnier in a theater with lots of people laughing around you." Another one said, "When I saw *Broadway Danny Rose* (Woody Allen, 1984) there was this older woman sitting behind me, you know, the kind with the big pocketbook. Well in one scene Woody is eating in the Carnegie Deli and this lady turns to her friend and says 'I still think the corned beef is better at the Stage.' How can you overhear something like this in your living room?"[41] Some people prefer the large screen because, at home, telephone calls interrupt their viewing. I would not mention the grievances about the popcorn that doesn't taste the same when you pop it at home! I rather agree with Vincent Canby when he writes: "A horror film watched in a theater is a game. Watched when one is alone, in the kind of privacy in which one does a geography lesson (or shaves and showers), it assumes the importance of a disorienting daydream."[42]

Moreover many telling details of the mise-en-scène, which help to transmit the "meaning" of a movie, are lost on the small screen, especially in outdoor scenes. Thus, several of John Ford's westerns lose steam when watched on the television set. Claude Chabrol, when still a film critic, once told me that what constituted the "miracle of Hollywood cinema" was the "detail" that caught the attention of the spectators and helped them to understand the subtleties of the characters and the intentions of the director. This remark was proffered by Chabrol, if I am not mistaken, after we had seen *Rear Window* (1954). Chabrol was referring to some gestures by Jimmy Stewart and the way he was handling his camera. Obviously, such details escape the TV viewer's attention. Hence, the numerous close-ups in films directly produced for the small screen. Hence, also, the importance of speech, not only in talk shows and news programs, but also in soaps and prime-time sitcoms. Dialogue is as essential (if not more so) as image in TV narrative style. Today scripts written for either TV or cinema abound in explanatory dialogue. This is due to two key facts: First, screenwriters are working in both media, and, second, films are no longer destined solely for theaters. Instead, they end up for very long periods (if not forever!) on the small screen. While the plethora of speech seems acceptable on the TV screen, it becomes boring on the large one! From this angle, TV is nearer to the theater. Teleplays are more plays than film material. For the same reasons, we find a growing tendency toward abuse of close-ups in today's movies. (This is probably unconscious on the part of directors; but those who have worked for both media tend to be egregious in their use of closeups! We find this, for example, in Sidney Lumet's movies; indeed, he started his career in TV.)

In the present state of technology, television retains a quality absent from cinema: *instantaneity* or, if one prefers, *immediateness* (in live shows and news). In relation to this, I would like to describe here a very personal experience. This occurred in May 1969, in Manhattan, exactly on the nineteenth. I was sitting in front of the small screen of my television set, waiting to see the picture of our earth sent back directly from Apollo 10. Suddenly, the blue globe, flecked with white specks, loomed before my eyes. An indescribable feeling took hold of me. There I was, sitting in my room on earth, and yet at the same time I was observing my planet from the outside, as if I were in the spaceship that was sending back the image! And even more extraordinary: At the same time I was also present in the picture I was looking at, and this at that very instant! Technology had made possible such an incredible feat!

Obviously such a "two-way" instantaneity doesn't happen often. But one-way instantaneity, if I may say so, is a common feature of television. This relatively recent medium is somehow ubiquitous, almost omnipresent! It seems to proclaim: "Everywhere, NOW!" André Malraux once wrote, "A film on architecture might show Beijing's 'Forbidden City,' but the latter would always pop on the small screen at the death of a Chinese leader." He added that television bestows on the "real" the glow of the "imaginary." He also underscored the difference between the spectators of cinema, theater, and television. In a theater the patron looks at the stage and in a cinema, at the screen; in both, their immediate neighbors look at them and judge their social rank according to their clothes. In front of the small screen, by contrast, each viewer is alone; nobody sees him because there is no audience, nobody speaks to him, not even the head of state who is addressing the nation. The viewer is able to impose silence on the head of state simply by switching the channel on which he is speaking or turning off the sound. The head of state will not be aware of this! Television is indeed "fantastic" in the literal sense of the word![43]

While I am talking about the relationship between television and cinema, perhaps it would be useful to add a few words on TV's effect on book reading. The book industry has not suffered very much from the invention and development of the animated image. Television has not (yet) "killed" cinema as some doom-sayers had predicted two or three decades ago. Nor has it effaced books and "killed" reading. On the contrary, reading is on the upswing, at least in Europe and Asia where special programs on books have rather helped the publishing industry! But as for cinema and books, the debate seems unending and continues to provoke sometimes bitter exchanges!

Coming back to the effects of television on films, one must remember that the rapid development of TV gradually cut the size of the filmgoing audiences. Large theaters had to close and were replaced by multiplexes. Both cinemas and TV stations needed more and more films to fill the theaters and TV airtime. Films of different types were developed for different audiences—children, teens, adults, and the like. At the same time advertising abandoned the big screen for the small screen. Theaters ceased to show newsreels and shorts. To make up for the two hours of spectacle, films stretched from 90 to 120 minutes (or more!). Hence, a slower pace in narration (compared to pre-1950 movies). Yet the 90-minute formula triumphed in TV feature productions in order to allow enough time for commercials. Longer stories were told in mini-series format. At any rate, all this created a tendency toward multiplying unnecessary images. I, for one, have developed imaginary scissors in my head and do imaginary editing while watching new movies! In my opinion, almost any current film could easily be cut by about fifteen to thirty minutes without damaging its coherence! Old movies had a quality of terseness that seems lost among today's filmmakers.

World War II, almost immediately followed by the Korean and the Vietnam wars, changed the mood and tastes of younger generations and therefore indirectly affected moviemaking. The changes in lifestyle at the end of the '60s and the new openness in sexual relations (at least in the West) have also pervaded movies. Few films are released without one or two "explicit" love scenes. I remember Truffaut telling me in the early '70s that he was enchanted about this new "candor." It is true that, as kids, we did not know much about sexual relations and, watching films, believed that mere kissing could make women pregnant! But the way sex is now shown, especially in American and European films, reminds me of what we called the "law" with regard to Egyptian and Indian productions. Both countries produce more than two hundred features every year for local audiences. Scripts are conceived in a way to allow at least three or four interruptions of the story for belly dancing and singing! No studio would invest in a story without such popular gimmicks. In 1960 I was in Rabat, Morocco, trying to while away a few hours between two planes. I spotted a film theater showing Egyptian movies. The box-office attendant told me that it was sold out. Yet the theater was empty save for a kid seated near the exit door. Noticing my amazement, the attendant explained that the ticket holders were smoking water pipes and drinking green tea in a nearby café. "They do not like the Egyptian story lines and do not understand Egyptian colloquial Arabic," he explained. "For a very small fee, the kid will inform them when dancing and singing sequences are on. They all rush in and afterwards returned to the café!"

It seems to me that European and American filmmakers have created their own "law": They interrupt all their stories, even the most suspenseful ones, two or three times to show people in bed or to allow pop singers to scream! Incidentally, this trend indirectly explains to a large extent the success of Iranian movies (and some other foreign films) in Western film festivals. Due to the mullahs' censorship, Iranian directors cannot show scenes of unveiled women or boys and girls kissing, much less love scenes. No more dancing, singing, flirting, or the like. Their films are so different that they earn the applause of the Western public! This is exactly what happened in the West in the '60s when Japanese movies by Mizoguchi and Kurosawa were shown in festivals! The tempo and the cinematography were so different from what was usually screened that the audiences gave them standing ovations. The same applies to the Indian director Satjiatit Ray. (These remarks do not mean to imply that Indian, Iranian and other countries' directors are talentless! To the contrary, some of them are first-rate filmmakers and can be considered as "auteurs.")

Be this as it may, it seems that once again Hollywood is in a funk, as if history is repeating itself. The average cost of a movie shot in the studios has more than doubled since the start of the last decade of the twentieth century. The *Wall Street Journal* reported on April 12, 1999 that "Megahits like *Titanic* aside, the major studios' average return on investment from movies slipped to nearly nothing over the past decade." In an article titled "Hollywood Chastened by High Costs, Finds a New Theme: Cheap," Bruce Orwall and John Lippman wrote that studios were cutting the number of films they produced, especially big-budget ones, and ditching hundreds of projects. Indeed, some actors command $20 million or more for a single movie and push up the salaries of technicians and directors in their wake, inflating the already high costs. So the ensuing slowdown is perfectly understandable. Moreover, with the "digital" revolution and the more and more childish films, movies are becoming formulas without appeal to audiences demanding mature entertainment. The wheel is coming full circle and, once again, the industry is facing the same problems as in the '60s. Once again it must go after new talent, penny-pinching, artistic achievement, and catering to diverse age groups—unless the new technologies throw wool over the viewers' eyes!

21

Cyber Cinema?

It seems to me not only that movies are getting longer by the day but that they are also becoming more and more the work of cinematographers and editors than that of directors. That is, directors are becoming mere technicians among many others; therefore, they are losing the auteur quality my friends and myself were looking for in our approach to cinema in the '50s and '60s.

Let me illustrate this affirmation with some examples. The camera today often slows down and stops on scenery or faces for no particular reason except that they are nice to look at. Such films tend to become travelogues, presenting, so to speak, colorful "postcards" and bevies of models. Nudity abounds just because the female body attracts male—and sometimes female—spectators. What we used to call mise-en-scène in the 1960s tends to disappear.

Mise-en-scène has vanished from films produced for TV; in those, "direction" means to shoot the script as it stands and reduce the costs as much as possible. Most TV features and miniseries are flatly produced. At best, they are nice "photographs" illustrating a story! Indeed, today's cinema, especially in the framework of TV, does not need great directors. What we used to call auteurs' films have become an extreme rarity! Some of these films have no need for a director at all: They can be made with a scriptwriter and a cinematographer, sometimes just an apprentice-cameraman. That brings to mind a personal recollection. In 1956, while visiting a Cairo studio, I was told about a director who used to say to the actors after rehearsal: "You know what you have to do and you have memorized your lines?" The actors would nod affirmatively. Then the director would ask the cinematographer: "You have studied all the indications about angles and different shots as specified in the shooting script?" "Yes, sir." "Therefore," the director would conclude, "you don't need me. I am going to take a nap in my office. If you have a difficulty, call me!" I think that we are heading toward such a situation in TV film production and, if things continue as they are proceeding now, in cinema too.

Moreover, motion pictures and what is called "interactive entertainment" have an inclination toward cooperation if not merger. It has become easier to incorporate some of film's creative ideas into computer software. At the same time, computer software publishers are seeking to add "star power" to their products. The trend to use digital and computer technology as well as video technology is blurring the distinction between the big screen, the small screen, and the computer screen.

Several companies have begun "webcasting" short films and comedy bits. According to David Neuman, president of Digital Entertainment, "This is ground zero of a media revolution. What we're doing is as exciting in its own way as what D. W. Griffith got to do at the beginning of the motion picture industry" (cited by Bruce Orwall and Peter Gumble in "The Big Battle in Hollywood," *The New York Times*, October 28, 1999). The web moviemakers consider that in a not too far future, the Internet will become a viable competing vehicle for feature presentations and therefore a viable alternative to film theaters.

In any case, the rapid invention, development, and expansion of new technologies in the field of communications and entertainment, are already heralding further changes in filmmaking—

some of them fundamental. For instance, a new device called "plototronics," which is still under development, allows the viewer to change everything—the plot, the characters, the actors—at the push of a few buttons. According to Sam Quentin, the plototronics inventor, with a series of keystrokes on a personal computer, users will be able to construct stories of their own choosing, insert their favorite actors into actual movie plots and create a "holographic film."[44] Just imagine: Directors, scriptwriters, cinematographers, and actors would no longer be needed! All viewers would become directors! I, for one, am not afraid of such a development. Indeed, as I said earlier, everybody is and can be a film director, because everybody "directs" dreams every night!

But such new technologies raise problems of a different kind. For instance, it is said that in laboratory tests, technicians have been able to alter scenes in *Citizen Kane* (1940), including the opening one in which Kane's mother calls him. In the new version she says, "Come in here" and adds, "and bring that Rosebud sled with you"! This "corrected" version eliminates the "confusion" that marked Welles's movie about the word "rosebud"; at the same time it erases the "mystery" that triggered the journalistic inquiry that stands at the core of the story! Moreover, mishaps may happen, as in the case of a lab technician who erased the Holocaust from *Schindler's List* and made the hero the coach of a German soccer team! Today special effects wizards are capable of propelling any actor through a plate-glass window without messing up her hairdo!

Such a basic and total transformation of the whole process of filmmaking has not yet become the norm. But some steps have already been taken in that direction by special effects specialists.[45] Dennis Muren, who supervised the mechanical and optical effects in *Star Wars* (1977) has become an avant-garde specialist in digitally induced images. With his team, and using computer-controlled mechanical systems, he produced the high-speed chase in *Return of the Jedi* (1983), the walk of the dinosaurs in *Jurassic Park*, the chameleon android in *Terminator 2* (1991), and many other extraordinary sequences. Creating "digital" monsters is indeed a first stage on the road toward computer-conceived humans! Advocates of this trend are convinced that computers can create believable characters. In their opinion, the "digital power" that put dinosaurs on the screen can certainly, say, bring Marilyn Monroe back from the grave, or invent perfect "new" protagonists. *Digital* or *cyber* actors are around the corner![46] These "photo-realistic" *synthetic* actors are sometimes called "synthespians." According to their aficionados, novelties such as "virtual reality" (a computer-generated environment that participants interact with) and "interactivity" (the control of some computer-generated simulation), still in their infancy, will change the nature and role of viewers themselves in the not-so-distant future.

Already, "digital imagery" is gaining a toehold in film production. Not only it is used for special effects, but it also saves on costs by creating "virtual" sets from still photos. Building real physical sets is eight to ten times more expensive, as Nick Wingfield of the *Wall Street Journal* (November 16, 1998) reported in a special section on the future of cyber technology in cinema and other entertainment domains. It seems obvious that what my friends and myself in the 1950s and 1960s used to describe as "personal" cinema and "auteur" film, tend to disappear in this new technological environment. I think that not too far in the future, only one director's name will continue to shine in Hollywood's sky. Alan Smithee—whose trademark since the start of his directorial career in 1967 is that he has no distinguishable style—is a common pseudonym for directors whose films were taken away from them and heavily recut against their wishes. With the new advances of computer science and gadgets, directors are more and more losing a grip on their films!

Pundits say that *digital media*—from the World Wide Web to 3D video games, to unknown technologies to come—will soon exert a force as pervasive and powerful in the lives of the masses as film and television do today. They will bring us drama and diversions unlike anything we have previously known. They will change the way we think about entertainment and leisure.[47] According to David Bank who conducted a comprehensive inquiry into the digital media in 1997: "Though still in its infancy, the digital realm already is providing hints of what will please the crowds and what won't. The unifying theme is *interactivity*, the unique strength of digital media. Video is best on television, audio is best on radio, and text and photos are best in print. Only computers can integrate all of them, add instant access to information databases, and then let the audience play with the mix—and each other."[48] Attempts are being made at combining storytelling with participation. Bank speaks of *The Last Express*, a CD-ROM set aboard the Orient Express from Paris to Constantinople on the eve of World War I, in which the screenplay is like an invisible hand that "draws you along." The participants "can trigger major events."

The Spot, an online soap opera telling the story of five southern California housemates, provoked a sensation when it started in June 1995. It exploited the Internet's ability to involve audience members and take into account their reactions. Let's listen to Don Clark who participated in the above-mentioned inquiry: "*The Spot* tapped into a latent demand for narrative [on the Web]. People seemed to be caught up in the story of the beach house and its occupants, who had the physical attractiveness of TV's soap stars along with some high-brow Generation X insights."[49] At first members of the audience believed it was real. Even when they realized that the settings and the characters were fictional, they continued to provide advice through e-mail. Writers quickly incorporated their suggestions into the story. One wonders what will happen to the concepts of mise-en-scène and auteurs in the new environment that is dawning on the entertainment industry. The "interactive" cinema would be the work of many people both on the production and the audience sides! Already, the audience, without knowing it, is influencing the production as well as the content and direction of movies. Indeed, filmmakers have always tried to cater to the taste of the audience. Like many politicians (including the president of the United States), they consult polls, which are mainly concentrated not in the oval office but in the box office! In that sense, the new technology will only make the audience's influence more direct!

Yet another reporter participating in the inquiry, Lisa Bannon, describes "Willisville," a futuristic community that offers an example of the 3D worlds the Internet could provide. "By 'unloading' their own image, music and text, visitors can walk down the streets and into the stores and homes of the town's fictional characters, engaging in dialogue or otherwise becoming actors in a collision of high-tech and soap-opera kitsch."[50] But as one of the participants in the inquiry noted, "Even with the development of virtual worlds, text-based sites (on the Web) are likely to continue thriving as forums for impassioned conversations. They offer a way for devotees of almost any topic, no matter how narrow, to find one another and exchange thoughts."[51]

This last remark brings me back to the question that launched this book: the fate of books and print in the rapidly coming Cyber Age.

22

Are There Books in Our Future?

It is indeed difficult, if not impossible, to resist the lure of new technologies that are transforming our lives as well as our societies. I, for one, clung as long as I could to my typewriter, but by 1994 I could no longer deny the superiority and advantages of the word processor. And now I spend most of my time in front of my computer writing, wading through newspapers and magazines, reading long articles and stories as well as medium-sized books. Between the television screen and the PC window, I barely find time to read "normal" books. The computer age seems to herald an *epochal shift* from print to electronic media that will undoubtedly affect our entertainment habits. Once again, people wonder if books will exist in our future.

The French writer and film critic, Claude Mauriac, who died in 1998, exclaimed once, "Cinema will erase literature!" He was referring to what he called the powerful *presence* of images in our societies. Yet literature survived the onslaught of cinema and television. Although Mauriac and many novelists had to change their writing styles, literature survived! Other prophecies of doom have not materialized either, at least not yet. Thus, Marshall McLuhan's death sentence was not carried out: The "Gutenberg Galaxy" still lights up our societies' skies and the "typographic man" continues to read, though less than before. As for the poet Apollinaire's prediction, it still has a hundred years to go!

Judging from what happened since the invention and spread of cinema, television, and satellite communications, books seem to be a very stubborn commodity. In Ray Bradbury's *Fahrenheit 451*, they refuse to disappear and authorities have to decree their destruction! True, this was fiction; but real life, too, offers examples of books' resistance against the electronic tide. Thus, in 1997, I was struck by the experience of a small French village that, like many other European rural communities, was dying out. Its population had dwindled from 3,000 to less than 800. A few "book lovers" discovered it and set up shop in its narrow streets. Now it harbors no less than twelve bookstores and attracts yearly over 100,000 visitors![52] Such book villages also exist in England, Belgium, and some other European countries. Moreover, book reading doesn't seem in crisis, as local lending libraries and "used book" stores are growing in the United States and elsewhere.

To explain the staying power of books, Robert Darton, a professor of history at Princeton, wrote recently:

> Ever since the invention of the codex in the third or fourth century A.D. it has proven to be a marvelous machine— convenient to thumb through, comfortable to curl up with, superb for storage, and remarkably resistant to damage. It does not need to be upgraded or downloaded, accessed or booted, plugged into circuits or extracted from webs. Its design makes it a delight for the eyes. Its shape makes it a pleasure to hold in the hand. And its handiness has made it the basic tool of learning for thousands of years even before the library of Alexandria was founded early in the fourth century B.C.[53]

But such an almost poetic defense cannot resist the reality of digitalized technology. For one thing, printed matter can't move quickly enough to keep up with events. E-books (electronic) are expanding their realm. The New York Public Library recently reported 10 million "hits" on its computer system each month as opposed to 50,000 books dispensed in its reading room at Forty-second Street.[54] Enthusiasts of the Internet (sometimes called "cybercrats") affirm that the online world is a kind of limitless library that will make available to its users all the information, knowledge, literature, and entertainment ever produced.

Therefore the question is legitimate: Will there be books in our future?

Well, emulating President Clinton, I would say the answer depends on the definition of the word *future*. In the long term, as John Maynard Keynes once said, we will all be dead! In the immediate future, it seems that the printed word will continue to accompany us. Even Bill Gates, chairman and CEO of Microsoft, says that technology will have to improve "very radically" before "all the things we work with on paper today move over to digital form."[55] In addition, we know next to nothing about the effects of computers on health and especially on the eyes of users. It is therefore safe to say that, for the time being, books are not going to disappear into cyberspace as into thin air!

But what books are we talking about? Academic and scientific publications constitute a special category. What we are concerned with in the framework of this book is rather literature. I have previously indicated some of the effects of cinema and television on novels. Undoubtedly, new technologies will further affect them. In the opinion of some experts, they already have driven a wedge between readers and serious literature. That might be true if one looks at bestseller lists, which rarely carry important literary titles; but one should not forget that classics continue to sell quite well, if not at the pace of Danielle Steel and John Grisham titles!

In a 1989 collection of essays, the well-known critic Sven Birkerts complained that "electricity and inwardness are fundamentally discordant." He deplored the fact that attunement to the rhythms of MTV will preclude younger generations from responding to the patterns of great writers' prose.[56] What worried him even more was the coming loss of the very experience of reading. He wrote, "I value the state a book puts me in more than I value the specific content." What is this state? A special "process of immersion," of "double consciousness" of both the book's world and ours. But this can also happen in cinema, as I mentioned earlier when discussing the different ways of looking at the silver screen! Actually, the majority ´of spectators "immerse" themselves in the film's world and unconsciously compare it to their own! The phenomena of projection and identification are always at play. As I see it, only film critics should fight "immersion" and keep their distance from the movie in order to judge it as objectively as possible.

Sven Birkerts returned on the same theme in a more recent collection of essays (*Readings*, New York, 1999). He once again deplored the loss of a sense of mystery and a significant orientation toward the future—among both the readers and literature itself. In his opinion, this explained the brittleness and ephemerality of contemporary literature. Poetry is doomed because it requires profound attention. Following his line of thinking, one would conclude that Marcel Proust and Henry James, not to mention James Joyce, will become unread legends.

Birkerts is not the only one to deplore the dwindling of readership. In an essay titled "Square Peg," John Lippman deplored the "loss of knowledge" caused by the new technologies. He asserts that with speed and random access which are the "virtues" of cyberspace, we forget the patience to read slowly—"the most difficult kind of reading to learn." He concludes that "our information-obsessed age overruns knowledge and wisdom of the ages. Reading and the linear life, unlike surfing the Net, invites you to fill up the space around you with meaning. The value of mere information, in the end, is meaningless" (*The Wall Street Journal*, March 28, 1996). David Denby, a New York film critic who re-enrolled in a Columbia University humanities course, recounted his unusual experiment in a book. To his alarm, he admitted that he had been so conditioned by television, films, and popular culture that it was simply difficult for him to sit still for prolonged periods and read![57] As Raymond Sokolov, the Arts and Leisure page editor of the *Wall Street Journal*, once remarked, those who deplore the decline of books are prompt to round up the "usual suspects": cinema, television, and other electronic and chemical squatters in the youthful brains.[58] He added that the roots of the problem are deeper: incompetence of literature professors, the spread of post-modernist "deconstructionists," and so on. He recommended reading a book in which Robert Alter demonstrated the power and beauty of literature.[59]

In fact, the worries of some observers hide their nostalgia for the past. They are, as it were, afraid of abandoning long-established habits, afraid of erasing their sentimental attachment to booklike objects. They should perhaps listen to the advice of the novelist Margaret Diehl: "As for love of paper, my suggestion is to transfer it back to trees. Visit them, sniff their bark or a crisp curled leaf in October. The natural world is always with us. What matters in literature is the word" ("Ready to download now," in *The New Times Book Review*, December 12, 1999). The nostalgics forget that the world is in constant change and that humans always have to adapt to new circumstances. I never forget an exchange with my elder brother one afternoon after we had seen *You Can't Take it With You* (Frank Capra, 1938). I told him that I was sorry for our parents. "Why?" he asked with a touch of amazement. "There was no cinema when they were kids!" I couldn't imagine that people of the past could have been happy without the new forms of entertainment!

The rapid development of the new electronic technologies will certainly transform many things, as cinema and television did, respectively, in the beginning and the middle of the twentieth century. Books did not disappear but somehow changed. Novelists at the dawn of the twenty-first century no longer write like Balzac or Hemingway. They have even abandoned linear story-telling to the realm of film, no longer opting for new forms. To be sure, the new advances in communication will affect literature. But books will still survive, if only because cinema and

television need them and will continue to adapt masterpieces of
the past as well as non-literary contemporary stories. Literary
authors may explore new avenues and write differently and less
frequently than before. They may well become "cyber writers."
Nevertheless, classics will continue to be published and read. As
I indicated earlier, no film maker can ever reproduce the style
of Tolstoy or Faulkner. The genius of such authors lies not in the
stories they tell, but in the manner in which they present them.
And that manner is their exclusive property! Nobody can imi-
tate it.

At any rate, literature, if not books, will certainly survive in
the electronic age. Indeed, as noted earlier, literature and dreams
are very similar and both use the same narrative techniques but
not the same building blocks (images, words). In the future,
many authors will probably turn toward the new media. Those
who cannot find their way in the realm of electronics will write
and eventually publish. Moreover, at least on the basis of present
possibilities, film and electronics are not fit for scientific and phil-
osophical expression. For instance, neither cinema nor television
provide as broad an analysis of historical or scientific problems
as books do. A two-hour documentary simply cannot convey the
wealth of information contained in a 300-page book![60] Therefore,
it seems prudent to make a distinction between "book" and "literature" when one considers the question of the future of books
in an electronic environment. Cinema is as much literature as are
novels of the past and the present. The decline of books (if any)
might affect literature more than other domains.

Be that as it may, electronic books, which can be downloaded
to readers, will probably develop and eventually become a wide-
spread format. Already, different kinds of e-books are available.
Research is being conducted with an eye toward developing electronic paper and e-ink. In bookstores, with their limited shelf
space, old titles have to make room for new ones, causing many
books to go out of print within a few months. With books in
electronic format, text would be very cheap to store and distrib-
ute electronically and many titles would remain available for-

ever! From this perspective one can say that, far from "killing" books, the new technologies will actually help ensure their survival! A paradox? Only an apparent one. In order to dispel it, let me recount the story of Abdul Kassem Ismael, a grand Vizier of old Persia.[61] He was so attached to his 117,000-volume library that whenever he had to travel, he would have the books transported on a caravan of 400 camels trained to walk in alphabetical order! With a laptop-computer and an Internet link to all major libraries, he would certainly have avoided both the burden of maintaining a personal library of that magnitude and the cost of transporting it by such a long caravan!

There is still more to come in the relations between the electronic age and books. Take the views of Ray Kurzweil, a well-known software engineer and inventor, who predicted that a machine could become a champion chess player long before Gary Kasparov's defeat to IBM's Deep Blue. Kurzweil foresees a future in which there will be no conflict between humans and machines.[62] "We will be software," he proclaims. We will become immortals. And among the many advantages of this "new state," he cites the ability of reading any book in a few seconds! One would read Dante's *Inferno* in less time than it takes to brush one's teeth! A utopian dream? Certainly at the present stage of technology development! In the distant future? Who knows? The world of electronic communications is changing so rapidly that no one can predict what things will look like in even ten or twenty years from now. Kurzweil thinks that with sheer computational force, we can solve any "solvable problem." I am less sure of that than he is. I even doubt that we can ever solve the problem of the future of books, not speaking of the mysteries of the universe!

To Ray Kurzweil's unlimited optimism, I, for one, prefer Adam Hochschild's humorous prophecy in an article titled "On the Road Again" (*The New York Times Book Review*, October 17, 1999): "Some doomsayers these days claim that the book will soon be replaced by the computer chip. They're wrong—but only about the kind of doom involved. What will replace the

book is something else: the book tour. It's already happening."
At the end of his article Hochschild recounts the following story
from the novelist and historian JoAnn Levy, in the Internet magazine *Spotlight*: "In San Antonio . . . a Barnes and Noble store
asked twenty-three authors from a Women Writing the West
Conference to sign books at their store. Employees picked us up
at our hotel, had a huge horseshoe of tables, backed with 23
chairs, and 23 stacks of books next to place cards with our names
in calligraphy. Plus a big spread of cookies and coffee. Not one
person came! . . . After one hour we started buying each other's
books and then we ate all the cookies."

One more point before leaving this section. We should not
forget that, while sharing the same planet, we are far from being
all contemporaries. Some still live in prehistory, others in the
Middle Ages, in the eighteenth or nineteenth centuries! Such dis-
tinctions exist even in advanced countries between rich and
poor, educated and non-educated, and so on. It seems to me that
if books disappear in one place or in one group, they would
survive elsewhere or in another.

Marshall McLuhan's disciples believe that books have become
irrelevant. On the contrary, new developments clearly show that
every aspect of culture is relevant to every other aspect! Let me
therefore return to the realm of cinema, in light of the spread of
new technologies.

23

Cyber Narration: Shaharazad and Proust as Computer Programmers

I have already hinted at transformations in movies' narrative styles and mentioned some of their apparent causes, which range from changed sensibilities to new technologies. A number of experts predict still other, more revolutionary metamorphoses. Indeed, the Web is rapidly devouring the world of information and entertainment. Chat rooms are becoming three-dimensional. Video games allow hundreds of strangers to compete online against one another. Online magazines are multiplying and gaining sophistication. Online fictional worlds invite their visitors to become part of the action and even change the story! According to some analysts, the advent and development of the new technologies will exert as pervasive and powerful an influence on human lives as film and television do today! Computers and the Internet are even attracting artists.

"Working on the Web isn't like painting, which is more texture," says artist Joseph Squier to reporter Robin Frost "Nor is it like photography, which concentrates on detailed, accurate, precise images. Instead, the Web is more of a televisual medium. It's rawer, it's faster, it's about multiple layers of things happening simultaneously. Things move. It's an amalgam of still images, text, sound and moving images. It's a world in flux."[63] As

Frost explains, Web artwork might play with the orientation; using frames, the artist might divide the computer screen into segments, which might also be hyperlinks (clicking on them would allow the viewer to move through the work and also jump to another site). Frost adds, "Perhaps the most exciting aspect of Web art . . . is its interactivity, the relationship it sets up between the audience and the work." He quotes a professor of graphic arts who affirms that, in some cases, "Authorship becomes a joint project between the artist and the viewer."

Interactivity, audience participation, virtual reality (VR)— these are words and phrases that will invade our daily vocabulary for many years to come. They are concepts that will affect filmdom and other entertainment media. In this connection, I remember reading a book by Janet H. Murray, a professor of humanities and a senior research scientist at the Center for Educational Computing Initiatives at MIT, a few years back. It was called *Hamlet on the Holodeck: The Future of Narrative in Cyberspace.*[64] In Murray's opinion, computers were reshaping "the spectrum of narrative expression, not by replacing the novel or the movie, but by continuing their timeless *bardic* work within another framework." She predicted a future in which "cyberdramas" would reinvent storytelling as a "participatory" medium.

On narration, Professor Murray pointed out that novels, theater, and cinema are already abandoning the constraints of linear storytelling. Already they have begun to play with the possibilities of alternative realities. She cites movies such as *Back to the Future* (1985), in which the hero's tamperings with the past shape different futures, and *Groundhog Day* (1993), in which the hero relives the same day several times. Television shows like "ER" and "Homicide," too, already feature multiple plot lines and the *Rashomon technique* of telling the same story from different points of view has become an increasingly popular literary device.

Before examining her predictions in greater depth, I must point out that the themes of the above-mentioned movies had been used in science-fiction literature since the '40s—long before the advent of computers. Moreover, writers such as James Joyce rejected linear storytelling in the early years of the twentieth century. Finally, as to what she means by *Rashomon technique*, we should not forget that telling the same story by different persons was inaugurated some 2,000 years ago by the apostles in the Gospels; in filmdom, Orson Welles, to mention only one director, used it as early as 1940. On the "participatory" quality of "cyberdramas," I would be remiss if I did not quote Marcel Duchamp's celebrated line: "It is the viewer who 'makes' the work of art." Moreover, in an earlier section about viewing and making films, I underscored the extent to which spectators "project" themselves into movies and almost literally "make" or "deconstruct" some films, such as those of Antonioni! In modern theater, too, participatory plays have been produced since the mid-1960s, by such troupes as the Living Theater. In literature, we did not have to wait for post-modernist critics to appreciate the participatory role of the readers! As I noted earlier, narrative styles in literature and cinema interact with one another. In fact, the techniques of storytelling have barely changed. Over the centuries they have only been polished and improved. What is continually changing is the means of transmission of stories!

Having said that, I must recognize that Murray's foray into the "future of narrative in cyberspace" contains new dimensions and is, indeed, a very rewarding text. On the one hand, she forces the reader to reflect on the impact of electronic innovations on writing, filmmaking, and, in general, on the art of narration. On the other hand, tapping her considerable knowledge of literature and the performing arts, she draws some very interesting parallels between traditional literary forms and emerging electronic ones. For instance, practitioners of oral storytelling and *commedia dell'arte* share with computer programmers a reliance on formulas and stock characters.

Following her argument, I imagined Shaharazad escaping from the pages of the *Arabian Nights* and wandering through city streets at the start of this new millennium. I asked myself, What would she do to survive? She certainly would not spend 1,001 nights telling stories to a vicious tyrant suffering from insomnia.

The answer dawned on me almost immediately: She would become a computer programmer and a successful electronic author, selling millions of CD-ROMs around the world! I don't think that I am stretching my imagination too far. After all, not long ago a James Joyce enthusiast contended that, "At one level, *Ulysses* is a wonderful piece of software engineering."[65] And, from this perspective, what about Proust, Hugo, Tolstoy, and their peers? They were all "electronic authors" without being aware of it. They were computer programmers before the invention of the PC!

Electronic authors! This phrase reminds me of the case of the "novel written by a computer." This was in 1993. Scott French, an electronic surveillance consultant and computer programmer, decided to have a programmed computer write a Jacqueline Susann–type novel (akin to *Valley of the Dolls*). He wrote about one-quarter of the prose himself; the computer wrote another quarter; the rest was a collaboration between him and the machine. Titled *Just This Once*, it was published in 1993 and reviewed in *USA Today* together with another book of the same genre (*American Star* by Jackie Collins). The novelist Thomas Clifford reviewed both books. His verdict: "If you like this stuff, you'd be much, much better off with the one written by the computer"![66] I don't know if this experience has been duplicated or not. But it reveals a lot about the coming electronic age.

In this section I have alluded to changes in today's film production involving the ever-expanding role of technicians. Film directors' grip on their films is gradually loosening. They are becoming one technician among others. The concept of the director as an auteur (as we defended it in the '50s and '60s) is definitely on the wane. The personal movies we lauded in those days simply are not made anymore. George Lucas exemplifies what is happening in contemporary cinema, especially in Hollywood. After the admirable and very personal *American Graffiti* (1973), he immersed himself as director or producer or both, in the high-tech *Star Wars* (1977), *The Empire Strikes Back* (1980), and *Return of the Jedi* (1983), which cannot be considered auteur films. From this standpoint, literature seems today more of an art than cinema. But, indeed, much less entertaining! Are new technologies sounding the death knell of film auteurism? I feel inclined to answer affirmatively, at least for the immediate future.

But let me return to the *Arabian Nights* and Shaharazad. Her royal husband used her as an insomniac would use a TV set! Indeed, people expect film and television to tell entertaining stories! The sultan would fall into a slumber before the end of the story and ask his talented wife the next evening to tell him what happened! (Actually, in a 1956 study published in *Cahiers du Cinéma*, I compared the structure of serials to Shaharazad's style of storytelling.) But more than acting like a "sleeping pill," Shaharazad's tales fundamentally establish the basic *entertainment quality* of storytelling. They underscore the importance of entertainment in humans' lives. Even the Bible, the Gospels, and the Koran tell stories! Moreover, the Bible reveals the "secrets of the trade"; indeed, it cites the importance of composition or arrangement in storytelling (what my friends and I called mise-en-scène in our film reviews) in the following passage of the "Apocrypha" at the end of the Second Book of the "Maccabees":

> If its composition is good and felicitous, that is precisely what I desired; but if it is mediocre and of little worth, it is all that was within my power to do. Just as, indeed, it is counseled not to drink wine alone or water likewise alone, whereas wine mixed with water is pleasant and provides a delicious pleasure, so too the *harmonious arrangement of the tale* charms those who read the work. This will be the end.

The end! Not quite yet for this book. The link between entertainment and storytelling as shown by the above quotation as well as by Shaharazad's skills in the *Arabian Nights*, goes back to the beginnings of humanity. It is as if entertainment were part of our basic needs. Consequently, I am amazed by the number of attacks directed against film, television, and now the Internet by some intelligent and learned people. I mentioned earlier Professor Neil Postman's *Entertaining Ourselves to Death.* I recently stumbled on another study of the same kind *Life, the Movie: How Entertainment Conquered Reality.*[67] Its author, Neal Gabler, recognizes that the "urge for entertainment" has always been "innate in human nature." But the "effulgence of junk" has invaded it and gained the upper hand.

Movies constituted the "ultimate cultural weapon." Replacing words with images, the movies and then television gave vivid, immediate, and seductive expression to people's longings. As a result, what Gabler calls "the life movie" or "lifie," became the "life" lived not only by celebrities but also by ordinary people. Image and fantasy are prized and honored; accomplishment is not. Whether people are on the screen (actors, celebrities) or in the audience, they all are in the show! To Gabler, "homo scaenicus" (the theater-man) has arrived in the Western world. He is a man whose very consciousness consists of the stories he invents for himself, in which real and unreal are mixed to such a degree that it becomes impossible to separate them.

Gabler adds that the rise of entertainment is the most significant social event of our time: We now live in a "nightmarish world" in which emotion triumphs over reason, chaos over order. "Low culture" is destroying the "high" one. (Although I have no intention of addressing the social consequences of film, I would like to recall that my fellow film fans of the '50s and myself never acknowledged the separation of culture in two groups, one loftier than the other.)

Be that as it may, virtual reality (VR) seems to trumpet a "revolution" of its own in the Internet—or information technology (IT)—revolution. Its impact on all forms of entertainment (and, indeed, our lives) is still open to discussion. It certainly forces us to redefine the boundaries of "reality" and "fiction." Difficult enterprise if not "mission impossible"! And, after more thinking, one wonders if IT itself is not a kind of VR, if, after all, we should not propose the equation IT=VR!

24

The Meaning of It All

To wind up this book, I would like to come back for a short moment to Shaharazad. As I suggested previously, her story-telling was linked to the insomnia of her royal husband. He probably could not have dreams or, like children, only the imaginary world of tales could drive him to sleep. Whatever the case, he badly needed the "virtual" setting of his wife's fiction. Here I borrow on purpose the adjective "virtual" from the new cyber-language. Indeed, computer-induced VRs are tantamount to the fictional worlds created by great novelists or filmmakers.[68] The anonymous compilers of the *One Thousand And One Nights* did not bother to clarify this aspect of their book. Nor did the scholars who analyzed the stories and wrote about them.

But whatever the sultans disorder and the relation of his wife's tales to his sleeping, his case brings me back to what I was suggesting about dreams at the outset; namely, that the ways in which dreams have combined "animated" images since the very beginnings of mankind constitutes the model for all forms of narration—literary as well as cinematic. Jean Cocteau used to say that dreams are the *literature of sleep*. Without belying the celebrated French author, playwright, and film director, I would rather state that they are *the cinema of sleep*. Indeed, the mechanisms of dream's elaboration, catalogued by Freud, remind one of the devices used first by writers and later by filmmakers to convey stories to their audiences. And in this respect Shaharazad was the greatest storyteller of them all. Entertainers, including the film industry, should honor her. Who knows? Maybe one day a statue will be erected in her memory in downtown Hollywood! Maybe one day she'll serve as a model for the coming cyberspace entertainment's "Oscar." But for the time being the entertainment industry is rather preoccupied by its dwindling incomes and the upheaval that new technologies are bringing to its realm.

Curiously enough, the changes in cinematic narration (abrupt cuts, rapid pace, etc.) seem to bring films closer to dreams. Dreams, after all, usually proceed in a hectic way, except that the dreamer, as opposed to the electronic age director, remains the sole author of his nightly productions! Our dreams, I firmly, believed, are meant to entertain us. And I remain convinced that all humans are born with the urge to entertain and be entertained, with the urge to communicate what they see or conceive, with the urge to tell or listen to stories.

We were always eager to find new ways or invent new contraptions capable of fulfilling these urges of ours. We first devised language; we used painting (as in the drawings on prehistoric cave walls and later on household implements, plates, mugs, vases, etc.). We then conceived writing (hieroglyphs, diverse alphabets, etc.). We composed books, duplicated by scribes. Many centuries later we developed printing presses with movable type. Later on, photography appeared, followed by the transmission of sound (phonograph, telephone). Radio recreated in modern terms the oral storytelling of yore. By the end of the nineteenth century, cinema appeared with the invention of movie cameras and projectors. By mid-twentieth century, television spread the images inside our living rooms. And now, at the dawn of a new millennium, computers, CD-ROMs, the Internet, and other new communications technologies are spreading electronic communications all over the planet.

The most surprising thing about this long succession of inventions is that they all share *the same purpose: transmitting (and at the same time storing) the thoughts and visions of individuals to their fellow human beings.* In fact, it seems as if these inventions were part of a more powerful and completely mysterious device whose blueprint is still in the making.

Indeed, most of today's rapid achievements look like successive "improvements" on already existing contrivances or, better yet, like new pieces of *one huge puzzle.* To put it in other words, I would say that the rapid succession of inventions we are witnessing appear as if they were consecutive stages on a *predetermined trajectory,* as if they all were directed toward *one definite objective.* Indeed, looking back at the novelties produced during the twentieth century in the domain of mass communications and the slower-paced innovations since prehistory, it seems to me that there exists a *hidden purpose* behind all these activities, namely "externalizing" (if I may say so) "internal processes" of the human mind. In this perspective, the invention of cameras and projectors allowed the production of "dreams" outside the human brain (whereas language and writing produced "dreams in words"!). The new technologies that followed can be considered merely as successive improvements and sometimes "forward" leaps in this continuing process (as what followed the printing press up to the last years of the twentieth century were improvements on Guttenberg's invention).

I would therefore submit that the development of communications technologies follows a clear and recognizable pattern. It aims at a formidable goal, hidden in the creases of man's imagination (or mind?), namely, *materialization* of the human brain's internal processes or, in other words, the external *projection of thoughts.* Such an ambition has preoccupied humans almost from their first appearance on the surface of earth. Science-fiction writers have tackled this subject for many years, if not for centuries. It was actually the theme of a relatively good and intelligent SF movie, *Forbidden Planet* (1956, Fred McLeod Wilcox), based on Shakespeare's *The Tempest.* In a sense, virtual reality (VR) is nothing more than a *simulation* of what might be called the *outer-projectional drive of humans*. Actually, a fantasy version of such a VR (or "projection" ability) was used long before the invention of computers in the film version of the madcap Broadway show *Hellzapoppin* (directed by H. C. Potter, 1941). When the fictitious director and scriptwriter discuss the plot and the characters, their ideas "materialize" on the wall before them, and some of the imaginary characters react to the insulting comments of their potential "creators"!

Then, what the future has in store might be easily predicted. It is not so much changes in narrative styles or invention of more rapid and powerful computers and related devices. Rather it is the discovery or invention of *a process allowing each of us to project our thoughts and dreams outside of our brains* for the benefit (or the annoyance!) of our fellow humans! In our dreams, daydreams, and musings, each of us conceive stories of which we usually are the hero (or the victim!). We cannot communicate all of them by transforming them into written or filmed versions because this would cost too much in terms of both money and time.

The real problem is not to assess the future of books, films, and other entertainment devices in a superwired planet. I would rather leave this to sociologists, economists, philosophers, and other academics. *The seminal problem* is to find the proper technology that would permit us, so to speak, to "internalize," to "absorb" the essence of the communication devices in each individual, the technology that would allow humans to *directly* project their thoughts and products of their imaginations outside their brains, without a recourse to complicated and expensive machines.

Such an achievement is considered impossible by almost all scientists and experts. Would it really remain limited to the imagination of science-fiction writers? I, for one, think it is feasable. Indeed, technological advances already promise new methods of beaming movies directly to viewers. "Digital projectors" (as they are called) have been successfully built and implemented. This new technology will, among other things, eliminate today's sprocketed film strips in favor of electronically stored movies! No longer would films need restoration, and producers would be able to beam them via satellite to theaters, skipping the expense of printing and shipping! Such unforeseen advances in the domain of projection stir hopes.

As I am following the news about the latest inventions and musing on the *hidden* purpose of developments in mass communications, I remember what the great film director Luis Buñuel once told our group of "cultists" and "film fans" at *Cahiers du Cinéma, Positif,* and other magazines in the 1950s during a visit to Paris. He said that we will reach the *peak of filmmaking* when we will be able to sit in a room, switch off the lights and project on a wall, directly from our brains and through our eyes, the stories that we conceive in our heads!

I am sure that, one day, technology will develop the revolutionary means to accomplish such a feat. Then film would become completely personal and reach the "essence" of auteurism. Then, everyone would be an auteur in the sense of the reviews my friends and I were writing in the '50s and '60s.

Then image would finally supersede word.

Or would it?

Notes

1. Alexandre Astruc (born in 1923), a young film buff, had just published in 1946 a successful first novel. He wrote about films in the weekly *L'Ecran Français* founded after the liberation of Paris. In August 1948, his article, titled "La Camera Stylo," made history. He contended that filmmakers should use the camera as a means of expressing their personal point of view like writers. His was the first step in the "auteur" theory. In 1948 he produced several shorts and later directed features such as *Les Mauvaises Rencontres* (1955) and *L'Education Sentimentale* (1961) after Flaubert's famous novel. He also was a frequent contributor in *Cahiers du Cinéma*. His article about "La Camera Stylo" appeared in *L'Ecran Français*, March 30, 1948.

2. Henri Langlois (born in 1921), a cinema buff, collected before World War II everything connected with the seventh Art: films as well as photos and theater programs. In 1945 he founded the "Cinémathèque" (Film Library), which grew to become a world center. During the war he saved many films the Nazis wanted to eliminate.

3. Guillaume Apollinaire, a celebrated French poet who died of his war wounds in 1918, loved cinema. He predicted the "end of books" in a 1917 interview published in *Le Pays*, June 24, 1917 and reproduced in his Oeuvres Complètes en Prose tome II, La Pléiade, Paris.

4. George Bernard Shaw. *Collected Letters. 1926–1950.* London.

5. "Seen the Film? Read the Book," *New York Times*, January 28, 1987.

6. Freud originally published his findings in *The Interpretation of*

Dreams in 1900. What interests me here is not his theory that dreams are attempts to relieve emotional tensions that interfere with sleep, but the "mechanisms" he enumerated and analyzed—condensation, the combination of different ideas into a single symbol; displacement; etc. Other characteristics came to light in Freud's study of dreams, such as allegory, symbolism, allusion, etc., which are often used by directors in filmmaking. In addition to Freud's book, one can usefully consult "The History of Psychiatry" by Franz Alexander and Sheldon Selesnick (New York, 1966), especially chapter 12; and *The Handbook of Dream Analysis* by Emil Gutheil (New York, 1966), especially chapter 2.

7. André Bazin's ideas are contained in the four volumes of *Qu'est-ce que le Cinéma?* (Paris 1959, 1960 and 1961). These volumes comprise important theoretical articles collected after his death. Many of these articles have been translated into English by Hugh Gray in two volumes published by the University of California Press under the title *What is Cinema?* (1967 and 1971).

8. New York, 1989.

9. "Velazquez, Plato's Cave and Bette Davis," *New York Times*, March 15, 1987.

10. Ibid.

11. "Leçons Americaines" (French translation, Paris, 1989).

12. "Quick Cuts: The Novel Follows Film into a World of Few Words," *New York Times*, March 15, 1999.

13. Fred R. Barnard was the national advertising manager of Street Railways Advertising, a sizable agency in the 1920s *Source*: Burton Stevenson in *The McMillan Book of Proverbs, Maxims, and Famous Phrases*. Barnard's phrase first appeared in "The Printer's Ink," December 8, 1921.

14. Entry in his diaries, dated June 24, 1955.

15. Louis Ferdinand Céline, "Romans," tome IV (La Pléiade, Paris 1991).

16. Dudley Andrew. "André Bazin. Foreword by François Truffaut" (New York, 1978) This is the best and most accurate book I have seen in English about Bazin. Andrew, who teaches cinema at Iowa City University, gives both a biography of Bazin and an analysis of his views.

17. André Bazin. *What is Cinema?* 2 vols. Berkeley: University of California Press, 1967, 1971.

18. Ibid.

19. *Journal, 1942–1945* (Paris, 1989). Entry date: Monday, May 25, 1942.

20. *Great Directors at Work: Stanislavsky, Brecht, Kazan, Brook* (New York, 1986).

21. Cited by Zbigniev Osinski in *Grotowski and His Laboratory*, edited and translated by Lilian Vallee and Robert Findlay (New York, 1986).

22. *New York Times*, July 24, 1977.

23. "The New Review" (Paris, 1931–1932). I received this source from my friend, Basil Langton, a long-time theater director, actor, artist, and writer with whom I often discussed ideas developed in this book.

24. *L'Ecran Français*, March 30, 1948.

25. *Look*, November 3, 1970.

26. William Grimes, "The Auteur Theory of Film" in *New York Times*, February 20, 1995.

27. Schulberg was presented with a literary prize by the jury of the 1989 Deauville American Cinema Festival, for his scripts. His acceptance speech was condensed in an op-ed piece in the *New York Times*, of which a friend sent me a copy without mentioning the exact date! In a private conversation in the 1970s, Elia Kazan, who directed some of Schulberg's scripts, spoke highly of his talent.

28. "Auteur Auteur! The Movie Director as Star," the *New York Review of Books*, August 9, 1992.

29. *Nightmare of Ecstasy: The Life and Art of Edward D. Wood Jr.* (New York, 1992).

30. *Time*, June 1, 1992.

31. *Le Surrealisme au Cinema* (Paris, 1956).

32. *Look*, November 3, 1970.

33. "Cinéma et Litterature," special issue of *Cahiers du Cinéma*, 1966.

34. Lecture given at Radio City Music Hall, New York, on March 30, 1939. The event was organized jointly by the Museum of Modern Art (MOMA) and Columbia University. Transcripts can be obtained at MOMA. The interview was originally published by Peter Bogdanovich in his book *The Cinema of Alfred Hitchcock* (New York, 1963).

35. About the relationship between script and film, see chapter 9, "The filmmaker as author."

36. Jañet Maslin's review was published in the *New York Times*, July 12, 1996.

37. *Look*, November 3, 1970.

38. *Sacred Pleasure: Sex Myth and the Politics of the Body* (San Francisco, 1995). Riane Eisler is also the author of *The Chalice and the Blade* (1987).

39. *L'Homme Précaire et la Litterature* (Paris, 1977); especially chapters 8 and 11.

40. Stephen Hunter in *The Washington Post*, September 18, 1998.

41. Esther Fein in the *New York Times*, August 27, 1985.

42. "At Home the Story's Different" in the *New York Times*, February 2, 1988.

43. *L'Homme Précaire . . .*, op. cit.

44. David Blum, "Stardate 2005," section of the *Wall Street Journal*, September 15, 1997.

45. Frederick Rose, "Who Needs Actors," *Wall Street Journal*, September 15, 1995.

46. Ibid.

47. David Bank, "What Clicks," *Wall Street Journal*, September 15, 1995.

48. David Bank, "Clichés," *Wall Street Journal*, March 20, 1997.

49. Don Clark, "The Crucial Connection," *Wall Street Journal*, September 15, 1995.

50. Lisa Bannon, "Another World," *Wall Street Journal*, September 15, 1995.

51. Jared Sandberg, "Talk, Talk, Talk," *Wall Street Journal*, September 15, 1995.

52. Marlise Simons, "A Dying Village Is Fertile Soil for Bookworms," *New York Times*, July 30, 1997.

53. "The New Age of Books," *New York Review of Books*, March 18, 1999.

54. Ibid.

55. Ibid.

56. *The Gutenberg Elegies: The Fate of Reading in an Ideological Age* (New York, 1989).

57. *Great Books: My Adventures with Homer, Rousseau, Woolf and Other Indestructible Writers of the Western World* (New York, 1996).

58. *Wall Street Journal*, August 6, 1989.

59. *The Pleasure of Reading* (New York, 1988).

60. Nevertheless one can find exceptions as Steven Schecter's *Home Front* (1986) about World War II's impact on American life or the series *Nova*, both presented by PBS.

61. See Alberto Manguel, *A History of Reading* (New York, 1996).

62. *The Age of Spiritual Machines: When Computers Exceed Human Intelligence* (New York, 1996).

63. "Changing Picture," *Wall Street Journal*, March 20, 1997.

64. New York, 1998.

65. Robert Sullivan, "Virtually A-Wake," *New York Times Book Review*, June 16, 1996. According to the author, Joyce is the Internet's proto-stylist: "the author who anticipated the Web's stream of consciousness." He adds: "I like to think that Joyce, the man who attempted to open Ireland's first cinema, and the first significant mentioner of television in a work of fiction (from *Finnegans Wake*: 'Television kills telephony in

brothers' broil') would today have his own Web site—perhaps featuring Molly Bloom."

66. *International Herald Tribune*, July 3–4, 1993.

67. New York, 1998.

68. Stendhal used to compare a novel to a mirror the author places in front of the reader. Indeed, great authors in literature as well as in cinema create their own fictional worlds and invite readers or spectators to enter these worlds. Long after having read the novel or seen the movie, they remain enamored of it and recall the adventures of the characters they have mingled with!

Selected Bibliography

Ajame, Pierre. *Les Critiques de Cinéma*. Paris, 1967.

Allan, Kenneth. *The Meaning of Culture: Moving the Post-Modern Critique Forward*. New York, 1999.

Andrew, Dudley. *André Bazin*. New York, 1978.

Arnoux, Alexandre. *Du Muet au Parlant*. Paris, 1946.

Baecque, Antoine de. *Cahiers du Cinéma: Histoire d'une Revue*. Paris, 1991.

Baker, Christopher W. *How Did They Do It? Computer Illusion in Film and TV*. Indianapolis, 1994.

Barthes, Roland. *Critique et Verité*. Paris, 1966.

Basinger, Jeanine. *Silent Stars*. New York, 1999.

Battock, Gregory. *The New American Cinema*. New York, 1967.

Bazin, André. *What is Cinema?* 2 vols. Berkeley, 1967–71.

Birkerts, Sven. *The Gutenberg Elegies: The Fate of Reading in an Ideological Age*. New York, 1989.

———. *Readings*. New York, 1998.

Bogdanovich, Peter. *Pieces of Time: On the Movies*. New York, 1973.

———. *Fritz Lang in America*. New York, 1969.

———. *John Ford*. New York, 1968.

———. *The Cinema of Alfred Hitchcock*. New York, 1963.

———. *The Cinema of Howard Hawks*. New York, 1962.

———. *The Cinema of Orson Welles*. New York, 1961.

Boussinot, Roger. *Encyclopédie du Cinéma*. Paris, 1967.

Brook, James and Iain A. Boal, editors. *Resisting the Virtual Life: The Culture and Politics of Information*. San Francisco, 1995.

Burch, Noel. *Une Praxis du Cinéma*. Paris, 1986.

Callow, Simon. *Orson Welles: The Road to Xanadu*. New York, 1976.

Caughie, John. *Theories of Authorship*. London, 1972.

Charyn, Jerome. *Movieland: Hollywood and the Great American Dream Culture*. New York, 1986.

Chomsky, Noam. *Language and Mind*. New York, 1968.

Christopher, Nicholas. *Somewhere in the Night: Film Noir and the American City*. New York, 1997.

Ciment, Michel and Jacques Zimmer. *La critique de cinéma en France*. Paris, 1997.

Cohen-Seat, Gilbert. *Essais Sur les Principes d'une Philosophie du Cinéma*. Paris, 1958.

Debord, Guy. *Commentaires Sur la Société de Spectacle*. Paris, 1988.

Debrix, Jean-R. *Les Fondements de l'Art Cinématographique*. Paris, 1960.

Deleuze, Gilles. *Cinéma: L'Image-mouvement*. Paris, 1983.

―――. *Cinema: L'Image-Temps*. Paris, 1984.

Denby, David. *Great Books: My Adventures With Homer, Rousseau, Woolf and Other Indestructible Writers of the Western World*. New York, 1996.

Dennis, Everette E. *Reshaping the Media: Mass Communication in an Information Age*. Ann Arber, MI: Sage Publications, 1989.

Dickinson, Thorold. *A Discovery of Cinema*. London, 1971.

Doherty, Thomas. *Projections of War: Hollywood, American Culture, 1941–1945*. New York, 1993.

Eisenstein, Serguei. *Le Film, Sa Forme, Son Sens*. Paris, 1949.

―――. *Film Sense, Film Form*. New York, 1957.

Eisler, Riane. *Sacred Pleasure: Sex, Myth and the Politics of the Body*. San Francisco, 1995.

Falsetto, Mario. *Stanley Kubrick: A Narrative and Stylistic Analysis*. New York, 1994.

Fellini, Federico (with Tonino Guerra). *Amarcord: Je me Souviens*. Paris, 1973.

Fernandez, Dominique. *Eisenstein*. Paris, 1975.

Forester, Tom. *High-Tech Society: The Story of the Information Technology Revolution*. Cambridge, Mass., 1991.

Freud, Sigmund. *The Interpretation of Dreams*. New York, 1950.

Gabler, Neal. *Life the Movie: How Entertainment Conquered Reality*. New York, 1998.

Gelmis, Joseph. *The Film Director as Super-Star*. New York, 1970.

Gilder, George. *Life After Television*. New York, 1992.

Gillain, Anne. *François Truffaut: Le Secret Perdu*. Paris, 1991.

Gonzales, Christian. *Le Western*. Paris, 1979.

Graham, Peter. *The New Wave*. New York, 1972.

Grinsberg, Milton Moses. *Coming Apart*. New York, 1969.

Grotowski, Jerzy. *Towards a Poor Theater*. Denmark, 1968.

Hammond, Paul. *The Shadow and its Shadow: Surrealist Writings on Cinema*. London, 1978.

Hillier, Jim editor. *Cahiers du Cinéma: The 1950s*. New York, 1985.

———. *Cahiers du Cinéma: The 1960s*. New York, 1986.

Hobson, J. Allan. *The Dreaming Brain*. New York, 1998.

Hollander, Ann. *Moving Pictures*. New York, 1998.

Hudson, Liam. *Night Life: The Interpretation of Dreams*. New York, 1986.

Johnston, Carla Brooks. *Global News Access: The Impact of New Communications Technologies*. New York, 1998.

Kael, Pauline. *I Lost It at the Movies*. New York, 1965.

Kaufelt, David. *Midnight Movies*. New York, 1980.

Kauffmann, Stanley. *A World on Film*. New York, 1966.

Kreimeir, Klaus. *The UFA Story: A History of German's Greatest Film Company 1918–1945*. New York, 1997.

Kurzweil, Ray. *The Age of Spiritual Machines: When Computers Exceed Human Intelligence*. New York, 1996.

LoBrutto, Vincent. *Principal Photography: Interviews with Feature Film Cinematographers*. New York, 1999.

Macdonald, Dwight. *On Movies*. New York, 1969.

Maghsoudlou, Bahman. *Iranian Cinema*. New York, 1987.

Manguel, Alberto. *A History of Reading*. New York, 1996.

Marcorelles, Louis. *Living Cinema: New Directions in Contemporary Film Making*. New York, 1973.

Martin, James. *The Wired Society: A Challenge for Tomorrow*. New York, 1978.

Martin, Marcel. *Le Langage Cinématographique*. Paris, 1962.

McCarthy, Todd. *Howard Hawks*. New York, 1997.

Metz, Christian. *Essais sur la Signification au Cinema*. Paris, 1972.

———. *Langage et Cinéma*. Paris, 1970.

Mitry, Jean. *Esthetique et Psychologie du Cinéma*. Paris, 1973.

Morin, Edgar. *Le Cinéma ou l'Homme Imaginaire*. Paris, 1958.

Monaco, James. *The New Wave*. New York, 1976.

Monaco, Paul. *Understanding Society, Culture and Television*. New York, 1998.

Mullahy, Patrick. *Oedipus: Myth and Complex*. New York, 1948.

Murray, Janet H. *Hamlet on the Hollodeck: The Future of Narrative in Cyberspace*. New York, 1998.

Negroponte, Nicholas. *Being Digital*. New York, 1995.

Nichols, Bill. *Movies and Methods*. Berkeley, Calif., 1976.

Perkins, V. F. *Film as Film*. London, 1972.

Pinker, Steven. *The Language Instinct: How the Mind Creates Language.* New York, 1994.

Postman, Neil. *Entertaining Ourselves to Death: Public Discourse in the Age of Show Business.* New York, 1985.

Pudovkin, V. I. *Film Technique and Film Acting.* London, 1929.

Rentschler, Eric. *The Ministry of Illusions: Nazi Cinema and its Afterlife.* New York, 1998.

Rhode, Eric. *A History of the Cinema: From its Origins to 1970.* London, 1976.

Riefenstahl, Leni. *A Memoir.* New York, 1993.

Ritchie, Michael. *Please Stand By: A Prehistory of Television.* New York, 1991.

Rohmer, Eric (with Claude Chabrol). *Hitchcock.* New York, 1979.

Roman, James. *Love, Light and a Dream: Television's Past and Future.* New York, 1998.

Romano, Dario F. *L'Esperienza Cinematografica.* Milano, Italy, 1966.

Rondolino, Gianni. *Roberto Rossellini.* Torino, Italy, 1989.

Ross, Lillian. *Picture.* New York, 1990.

Rowland, Wade. *Spirit of the Web: The Age of Information from Telegraph to Internet.* Toronto, 1997.

Samuels, Charles Thomas. *Encountering Directors.* New York, 1972.

Sarris, Andrew. *Confession of a Cultist On the Cinema 1955–1969.* New York, 1970.

———. *Interviews With Directors.* New York, 1967.

———. *The American Cinema.* New York, 1969.

Saturday Review. December 19, 1959.

Slouka, Mark. *War of the Worlds: Cyberspace and the High-Tech Assault on Reality.* New York, 1995.

Sontag, Susan. *On Photography.* New York, 1977.

Tornabuoni, Lietta, editor. *Federico Fellini.* New York, 1995.

Trow, George W. S. *My Pilgrim's Progress: Media Studies, 1950–1998.* New York, 1999.

Truchaud, François. *Nicholas Ray.* Paris, 1965.

Truffaut, François. *Films in My Life.* New York, 1978.

Truffaut, François, with Helen G Scott. *Hitchcock.* New York, 1982.

Turkle, Sherry. *Life on the Screen: Identity in the Age of the Internet.* New York, 1996.

Verdone, Mario. *Roberto Rossellini* Paris, 1963. (This book contains my piece titled "Notes for a Portrait.")

Vidal, Gore. *Screening History.* Cambridge, Massachusetts, 1992.

Wako, Janet. *Hollywood in the Information Age.* Austin, TX: University of Texas Press, 1995.

Wees, William. *Recycled Images*. New York, 1993.
Weinberg, Herman. *The Lubitsch Touch*. New York, 1968.
Wells, Alan. *Mass Media and Society*. New York, 1979.
Williams, Christopher. *Realism and the Cinema*. London, 1980.
Wollen, Peter. *Signs and Meanings*. London, 1998.

Name Index

Subject Index

About the Author

FEREYDOUN HOVEYDA has had a long and distinguished career as a diplomat, writer, and critic. From 1953 to 1955 he was a member of the editorial board of *Cahiers du Cinéma*, the world-famous French magazine that launched what came to be known as the "New Wave." Hoveyda wrote scripts and collaborated as a writer and assistant with Roberto Rossellini on several projects, including the film *India* (1958). He has published some fourteen novels and non-fiction books in Paris; his latest book in English, *The Broken Crescent*, was published by Praeger in 1998.